THE GREAT TRAINER'S GUIDE

How to Train (*almost*) Anyone to do (*almost*) Anything!

by

Sue Vineyard, CVM

Heritage Arts Publishing
1807 Prairie Ave.
Downers Grove, Il. 60515

ISBN # 0-911029-249
c. 1990 by Sue Vineyard
Revised: 1995

Published by:

Heritage Arts Publishing
8493 Chicory Court
Darien, Illinois 60561

HOW TO USE THIS GUIDE

I have tried to make this work as useful and usable as possible to accommodate the various learning styles, needs and preferences of readers.

If you have read any of my previous books, you will immediately see that it varies from them in that it mixes two styles:

>   1. Text oriented (such as in *"Megatrends & Volunteerism"*)
>   2. Checklist oriented (such as in *"101 Ways to Raise Resources"*)

I assure you, the mix is intentional for several reasons: There are already tons of books by such heavyweight authors as Malcolm Knowles on adult education, and so I have avoided lengthy dissertations on andragogy vs. pedagogy, educational and training theories, curriculum development and seminar processes, etc. The bibliography can lead you to such works.

Do not misunderstand, all those theories are within the covers of this guide, but they may be hiding in more simple wordings, lists, suggestions or even light-hearted references that bring those theories, systems and processes into action statements.

Also, I know how busy you are, and reading another 300 page monster on the subject of training is probably not high on your "to-do" list for today!....thus the list format in my favorite "cut to the chase" style of writing.

I've also inflicted a personal idiosyncrasy of mine as I read books...I jot content notes in the margin so that I can leaf through the work later and easily spot topics and subtopics quickly, without having to read an entire section to locate one particular subject I'm looking for. Thus you will find content topics noted in the left margin throughout the guide.

All of this is aimed at making this work as "user-friendly" as possible. I can say, with some degree of certainty, that this format must have worked to a strong degree as this book's first edition has become the reference of choice of many nonprofit and public programs which must train volunteers and staff and now, in this revised format, it has become very popular with corporations challenged with training new staff on a constant basis.

Training was, for a number of years, my primary occupation. It allowed me to interact with up to 10,000 adults as I presented seminars of a few hours or a few days on topics as diverse as management and wellness, motivation and marketing. Today training takes a backseat to my work as author and consultant, but does not in any way dim my love of guiding audiences toward new discoveries and insights.

Training is hard work, but it is so rewarding that I hope you heed its call for many years to come. The world needs good, honest, well-informed and passionate trainers.

I hope this helps you be all of those things.

>   Sue Vineyard
>   1995, Revised

To Wes, the dearest one of all.

Acknowledgements

Many thanks to those who helped: Sandy Kueltzo, the world's greatest Administrative Assistant, master-typer and all around great cheerleader; Arlene Schindler, a teacher at so many levels of my life; Steve McCurley, great partner and trainer, Donna McGranahan, graphic designer and master "I'll-take-it-from-here, Sue" person, and a cast of thousands who have sat in my workshops and offered me guidance, learning and inspiration through the years.

Thank you all.

INDEX

INTRODUCTETTE

Introductions of books are usually long, ponderous and skipped over by the reader because they want to get to the meat of the work. Reading hundreds of words by the author about how they came to write the book, all their experience that validates it and how much this book will mean to the development of the world is often fluff the reader can do without.

In dwelling on these factors for about 4.2 seconds and understanding that you are at LEAST as busy as I, I decided to create a new style of Introduction, cleverly entitled "Introductette". It goes like this:

1. I've been a trainer professionally for 20 years . . . up to then training duties seemed to come attached to every job I took, paid or volunteer.

2. Evaluations have come back from the thousands I've trained averaging probably a 9.? on a scale of ten. Not bad.

3. I've accumulated lots of tips, thoughts-in-the-night and information on training adults. Do with them as you please.

4. I've authored 10 books and so decided to create an 11th. This is it.

5. I think a part of being a great trainer comes in the genes, but that which can be learned is probably somewhere between these covers or those of the books I reference.

6. I believe in training. Passionately. I think sharing information changes the people who then can change this world for the better.

7. I hope this guide helps. If it doesn't, please write your own. We need it.

8. Don't ever believe your own press clippings or take yourself too seriously. It has ruined a lot of good trainers who then felt themselves eligible to be Cannonized and have fan clubs in Peoria. Phooey.

And thank you for your support.

Sue Vineyard

CHAPTER 1

AN OVERVIEW OF TRAINING

Recent articles in newspapers, magazines, trade journals and a survey sent to nearly 3,000 professional managers of volunteers[1] all point to a growing interest in good training. Training budgets and openings for trainers in business, industry, government, nonprofits, education, service companies and organizations are increasing, which can only be interpreted to mean that the respect for and belief in training is solidly grounded and not a "flash in the pan".

Leaders from all corners of our world have come to understand that better things can be accomplished when people are trained to do tasks effectively and efficiently. Couple this new-found awareness with the increasing value of time as a precious commodity and you have a rich climate for growth in training as people ask to be equipped to do specific tasks rather than spend their valuable time learning by trial and error, or, more often, seat-of-the-pants and "Oops!" education.

Admittedly, this author is prejudice on the subject, but I believe there is no more critical or fundamental aspect to any effort than proper training to enable people to be successful. This does not mean that 50% of workers' time is spent in a classroom listening to some trainer drone on, but it does mean that on-going exposure to learning needs to be a part of any manager's overall plan for growth.

It's this simple:

✦ PEOPLE WANT TO DO A GOOD JOB & BE SUCCESSFUL . . .

✦ TRAINING EQUIPS THEM FOR SUCCESS & SATISFACTION . . .

✦ WHEN PEOPLE ARE SUCCESSFUL, THE ORGANIZATION OR EFFORT IS SUCCESSFUL . . .

✦ THIS AIDS WORKER RETENTION & ATTRACTS NEW PEOPLE & SUPPORTERS WHO . . .

✦ WANT TO DO A GOOD JOB & BE SUCCESSFUL . . .

And so the cycle is begun again.

Too often, however, the critical step of training is omitted, poorly planned, inappropriate or short-changed.

In this book you will find the various pieces that go into designing, implementing and evaluating good training. You'll also find tips that come from 20 plus years of training experience and several choice words about the role of the trainer . . . a rather critical part of the training package. Between all this is my own philosophy of training that refers to rather un-definable things like "passion", "caring" and "fun".

If you are looking for a heavy, doctoral thesis on training that reflects a somber importance of the subject, I suggest you head to your local library or university and check out any book on the subject weighing more than 10 pounds. This little piece is intended to challenge your "ah-ha's", reaffirm what your own good sense has taught you through the years and even, on occasion, tickle your funny bone (oh my!).

WHAT IS TRAINING, ANYWAY???

Webster goes on for a fourth of a page on what training is, and includes words that are fascinating when first contemplating what training really is:

"To lead or direct the growth of; to form by bending or pruning; to form by instruction, discipline, drill, etc.; educate narrowly; to teach so as to be fitted, qualified, proficient, etc.; to make prepared; to form habits or impart proficiency by teaching."[2]

Ida Rush George in her book *You Can Teach Others*[3] defines training by saying "Training improves one's job performance in the present job, in a job one has just been selected to perform and in a job one is being promoted to perform."

Malcolm Knowles, top guru in adult learning, states that "truly artistic teachers of adults perceive the focus of responsibility for learning to be in the learner; (he) conscientiously suppresses (his) own compulsion to teach what he knows (his) students ought to learn in favor of helping (his) students learn for themselves . . ."[4]

Elaine Yarbrough, PhD and Paul Friedman, PhD, in their book *Training Strategies from Start to Finish* say: "Training creates a bridge from the status quo to the desired state of affairs by providing appropriate learning experiences."[5]

Many authors try to help us grasp the meaning of training by distinguishing it from two other terms, education (defined as an improvement of "one's competence in areas beyond the present job that prepares the individual for increased or different responsibilities in the organization")[6] and development ("prepares one to grow and change as the organization grows and changes").[7]

As a trainer, I have come to believe that all of the above is correct, but none exclusively.

TRAINING

Training is a mixture of leading and directing the growth of people by educating, developing and teaching so that they can be more effective and proficient. It equips for the short and the long run, offering skill building that can provide immediate success and on-going satisfaction. Often it can provide life-skills that can be applied over and over again in different settings, promoting self-confidence, effectiveness and even wellness.

In short, training is whatever it is needed to be to accomplish immediate success and/or life-long satisfaction. It is pertinent, practical, "user-friendly" and sometimes even fun. It's goal is to improve, not to impede; to assist, not arrest. Sometimes it needs to change things, sometimes not; sometimes it needs to impart great technical detail, other times to simply get one great message across. Often it is more about encouraging people than educating them so that they will do the work, not because they have been given great secrets of implementation but the faith in themselves to do it.

WHAT TRAINING IS NOT

In looking at good training it is also important that we take a peek at what training is not to clarify it's real mission.

Training is not simply a platform for a trainer to wallow in self-grandizement. If all you hear from a trainer in a session is how wonderful he/she is and how smart they were when they ran a program, you might want to step out for a cup of coffee . . . they are not there to teach or instruct the audience, they are there to chalk up another standing ovation.

Training is not a format aimed at the sale of products... that is an insult to trainees, who came in good faith to learn and share, not to dig into their wallets before being allowed to leave.

Training is no guarantee of success for everyone in attendance. Communication is an imperfect science at best, and what the trainer says may not be heard by everyone. Sad as it is to admit, Mazlow was correct when he said, in discussing motivation, that "refusal to learn is more deeply a refusal to do."[8] On occasion, (rarely, thank goodness) the goal of a trainee is to negate what you are saying in a training. Being able to say "I just don't get it." after the 39th explanation by an exhausted trainer translates into: "I just don't want to do it". (A strategy I should have employed when Mother taught me how to clean an oven when I was 12!)

Even when attendees are sincerely trying to learn, some may honestly not "get it". If you know anything about left and right brained people, you understand that people who are rooted in their left-brain (logic, math, sequence, factual, etc.) will have a hard time in a training that is trying to impart "kinder, gentler organizational climate" by touchy-feely exercises (right brain thinking). They want to learn, but the training techniques turn them off and they come close to a nervous breakdown when the trainer admits there is no written agenda, handouts, overheads, lecture etc. . . . just an exercise that requires lute music, bare feet, a chiffon scarf and something about dancing with the cosmos!

Training is not a one-shot project. Bringing in new workers, sitting them down for 2 hours the day before they are to begin their work and giving them the history of the organization and a handout on their duties, does not constitute a training program. An effective training component in any program includes an orientation, on the job education, coaching, consulting, peer learning, skill building and many other forms of information sharing and teaching.

For every hour of formal training, another needs to occur in on-going skill building and development in informal ways or at least less structured. Training, therefore, need to be seen as a process rather than events that can be counted.

It needs to be user-oriented in balance with the needs of the organization so that expectations and goals can be achieved. To be sound and on-going, it must have it's roots in an agency-wide commitment to quality and integrity plus an honest belief in it's importance and value.

TRAINING
IS

Training is the cement that holds together a bridge that connects a dream to it's reality in any setting. It provides good people with good learning via good trainers who care passionately about the quality of the training and the skill building imparted to the trainees. The goal is success . . . for participants . . . for the organization and the trainer.

When done well, everyone wins!

WHERE TRAINING "FITS" IN MANAGING FOR SUCCESS

In order that training can meet the needs of the various unique individuals toward which it is geared, we must understand where it fits in management and recognize it's variations.

We must see it as an on-going process while still recognizing it as one of the ten components of management. Like planning, it has a definite placement in the sequence of management efforts and yet needs to be a fluid participant in all of the other aspects of the sequence.

In looking at it's place in the sequence of management, I use again my "Management Bridge" which shows the five functions and ten components which bridge the gap between our dreams and their realization . . . from what we envision as happening to seeing that vision come to be.

MANAGEMENT
BRIDGE

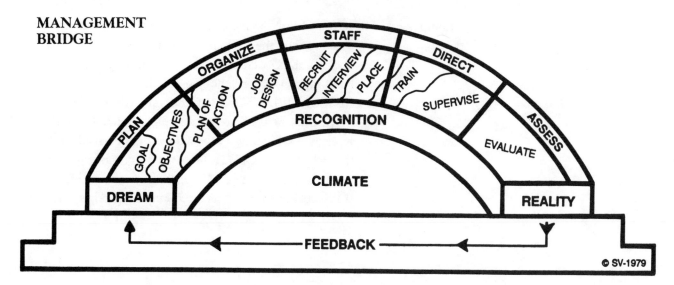

THE MANAGEMENT PROCESS

The management process begins with a dream or vision. It begins to build toward seeing that vision become a reality by following the 5 functions of management:

    1. Plan.

    2. Organize.

    3. Staff.

    4. Direct.

    5. Assess.

Incorporated in these 5 functions are their 10 components:

PLAN

A. PLAN

Component #1: GOAL: a statement of what is to be accomplished, the vision clarified.

Component #2: OBJECTIVES: they break the Goal into manageable pieces that are SPECIFIC, MEASURABLE, ACHIEVABLE and when accomplished, COMPATIBLE with the vision so that they will work together to make the Goal happen.

ORGANIZE

B. ORGANIZE

Component #3: PLANS OF ACTION: they break down the Objectives into bite-sized pieces that sketch out TIMELINES for efforts, WHO is needed (not necessarily by name but by special skills & numbers), WHERE they will be needed and HOW they might do the work.

Component #4: JOB DESIGNS: give even more specific information that lays out the various things that will need to be done for the Goal to be achieved . . . they tell the person who takes the job: the job TITLE, who they are RESPONSIBLE TO, what they are RESPONSIBLE FOR, what SKILLS are needed, how much TIME the work will take, how LONG they will be asked to do this job, what SUPPORT they will get and general information or PARAMETERS that affect this job (rules, background, history, accountability, budget, etc.).

STAFF

C. STAFF

Component #5: RECRUITMENT: this component brings all of the previous information together for use by the recruiter who uses it to target people who might be able and willing to take on the various jobs needed to accomplish the Goal. Within recruitment are the principles of motivation, marketing and the art of asking.

Component #6: INTERVIEWING: this is the art of targeted conversation and communication that provides information **to** a recruit and **from** them; it explores the potential for a match between specific people and jobs.

Component #7: PLACEMENT: this is the point at which people are offered and accept a particular job that satisfies their desires and meets the needs of the organization . . . it is "right people in right jobs".

DIRECT

D: DIRECT

Component #8: TRAINING: this is the formalized place in the Management Bridge for the TRAINING component. It is here that new recruits who have been assigned specific jobs acquire the information and skill building they need to begin their job successfully. The training may consist of a general **Orientation** followed by **Instructions** geared only to their particular work, or may offer other learning **Options** appropriate to the needs of the trainee or agency.

Component #9: SUPERVISION: this is the on-going effort by the supervisor to lead and manage the worker toward success. It embodies clear communication, fairness, respect, vision, support, flexibility and appropriate management. To be truly effective, it is cooperative, collaborative and coordinated (and on occasion, even fun!).

ASSESS

E: ASSESS

Component #10: EVALUATION: this is the component that allows everyone involved to assess and celebrate their successes and note those areas which allow for growth and adjustment to feed into future successes. Geared toward actions and efforts rather than individuals, it sets the stage for learning and is NOT a dreaded time for scolding.

RECOGNITION   Under-girding this Management Bridge that has spanned the distance between a vision and the realization of that vision, is the foundation of continual recognition of those involved in the effort. Rather than a singular event, plaque or letter of thanks, it too, like training, is an ongoing process that can be part of all the steps in good management.

FEEDBACK   The feedback of learning flows back to future dreams and actions as people learn from their experiences and factor them in as they repeat the management process or begin to work on new visions and dreams.

As you can see, TRAINING does indeed have it's specific place in the management sequence, but, because of it's critical importance, is also a subtle part of all of the other components and efforts that go into the successful accomplishment of every goal or vision of the organization. The following section shares just a few of the times training wears a disguise.

WHEN TRAINING WEARS A MASK

If we define training as an effort to equip people with the information, skills and tools for success, then we begin to recognize training opportunities inherent at many points of contact.

Training is part of the ongoing challenge to manage and lead people effectively. When people are successful and therefore attain both personal and organizational goals, it is **often attributable to strong leadership and guidance.**

In examining outstanding programs, agencies and organizations, I have ALWAYS found an extremely high valuing and use of continuing education.

Rather than assuming that an orientation at the start, a cute manual and a day of "watch-how-we-do-it" exercises is sufficient, outstandingly successful programs see training and learning as an ongoing process that is blended into every possible aspect of management and leadership.

SUBTLE TRAINING OPPORTUNITIES

The following list offers settings and management intervention points that are opportunities for educating and training people for success:

1. **Public Speaking:** whenever anyone from an organization speaks in public telling audiences of their dreams, goals and efforts, they are really educating people and possibly setting the stage for future interaction and/or support.

2. **Recruiting:** when talking to people collectively or individually, recruiters become educators/trainers by sharing information.

3. **Interviewing:** offering specific information to build potential workers' (paid or volunteer) understandings of roles, expectations, goals, etc.

4. **Job Designs:** offer an opportunity to clearly define work to be done, goals, timelines, parameters, etc.

5. **PR:** helping the public learn about an effort, agency or corporation.

6. **Funding Appeals:** telling the story; educating others.

7. **Newsletters:** helping people understand the "doing" and "being" faces of an organization . . . the heart and brain of an effort.

8. **Exhibits, Literature, etc.:** a passive training opportunity.

9. **Supervising:** this offers on-going opportunities to train workers by direct instruction, coaching, demonstration, etc.

10. **Evaluation:** most effective when it reinforces what has been done well and shares skill building ideas to improve those areas that are deficient. **CAN ONLY BE SEEN AS POSITIVE LEARNING (TRAINING) WHEN FOCUSED ON ISSUES & EFFORTS, NOT ON PERSONALITY!

When people come to understand an expanded definition of training as an ongoing process of education that wears many hats, those of us who are trainers can help them . . . supervisors, PR staff, Speakers Bureaus, recruiters, etc . . . take advantage of the opportunities they have to turn contact into "mini" training sessions.

CHAPTER 2

The Trainer

When mapping out training and looking at the critical issues of planning, designing, implementing and evaluating, the most important aspect of successful training may be overlooked or under-appreciated.

That aspect is, of course, the **trainer.**

As I said at the start, it is not easy to train effectively . . . in fact, the easier it looks to an audience, the harder the trainer is probably working!

There is an on-going debate about which is more important, the material or the trainer. Like the debate regarding the primary importance of the script or the actor, it has no easy answers but this much is certain . . . if the material **and** the presenter are top quality, the chances of successful learning on the part of the audience are multiplied a thousand times!

In being present during hundreds of presentations and being part of various faculties that are training trainers, I have come to believe that a good trainer can take less-than good material and make it interesting by fleshing it out with their own information, but a bad trainer can ruin good material.

Think back to a presentation you have attended where you came away thoroughly disgusted with poor quality, then discovered that in reading the trainer's handouts, there really was good material; it was the poor **training skills** that got in your way of learning.

I can recall sitting in a workshop once on computerizing a volunteer program and thinking it was the worst presentation I'd ever seen. The trainer was not prepared, did not understand who his audience was (he kept referring to everyone as business owners), believed his goal was to sell his software product, used jargon unfamiliar to the audience and was angry as people asked basic questions. He had some handouts I did not read at the time but were, as I was shocked to find out later, really quite valuable.

The problem was not the basic information prepared for this trainer (it was good), it was that he had probably never looked at it, came in with little or no training skills and had not done his homework on the group. Good material - poor training.

On the reverse side of the coin, I've also sat in on a training that was wonderfully fun and entertaining but, in hindsight, had little or no substance at all. Great performer - no material.

TRAINER ROLES

The role of the trainer is a constant challenge. It is akin to being an orchestra leader having to pay attention to all of the parts simultaneously while maintaining control and direction of the whole. Like the conductor, trainers must keep in mind several dimensions at the same time:

1. What is being said presently.

2. How to bridge or fit this part into what had just previously been said and what will come next.

3. Making this "connectedness" smooth, easy and logical.

4. What the point is for each piece.

5. How the audience is receiving the message:
   a. if it's been understood, move on.
   b. if there are still too many puzzled expressions, what technique to use to clarify: asking questions? group exercise? more examples from the trainer? examples from audience? diagramming thoughts visually? etc. etc.

6. Which technique is best for what is being said now and what technique will be used for the next point so that there is a mix for variety.

7. Integration of needs of adult learners who are either verbally, visually or haptically (experientially) oriented.

8. The timeframe.

9. Room comfort, temperature, seating, etc.

10. Where they are in the agenda (near a break, coming to a close? etc.).

Since it has been said that Einstein was a genius because he could think in 7 directions at one time, you can see trainers have their work cut out for them with the 10 plus directions listed above.

In addition to all this, trainers are also having to work with their various roles, knowing when and where to jump from one to the other or project them simultaneously.

COMPETENCIES

The American Society of Training and Development (ASTD)[9] lists the following roles a trainer plays and presents them as a list of necessary competencies:

1. **Needs Analyst:** defines gaps between ideal and actual performance and specifies the causes of the gaps.

2. **Task Analyst:** Identifies activities, tasks, sub-tasks, human resource and support requirements necessary to accomplish specific results in a job or organization.

3. **Program Designer:** Prepares objectives, defines content, selects, and sequences activities for a specific program.

4. **Instructional Writer:** Prepares written learning and instructional materials.

5. **Media Specialist:** Uses audio, visual, computer, and other hardware-based technologies for training, education and development.

6. **Program Administrator:** Ensures that the facilities, equipment, materials, participants and other components of a learning program are present and that program logistics run smoothly.

7. **Instructor:** Presents information and directs structured learning experiences so that individuals learn.

8. **Group Facilitator:** Manages group discussions and group processes so that individuals learn and group members feel the experience is positive.

9. **Evaluator:** Identifies the extent of a program, service or product's impact.

10. **Transfer Agent:** Helps individuals apply learning after the learning experience.

11. **Marketer:** Sells training, education and development viewpoints, learning packages, programs and services to target audiences outside the marketer's work unit. (In-house trainers also have to do this INSIDE their own organization).

12. **Theoretician:** Develops and tests theories of learning, training, education and development.

13. **Individual Development Counselor:** Helps an individual assess personal competencies, values and goals; also helps to identify and plan development and career actions.

14. **Manager of Training and Development:** Plans, organizes, staffs, controls training, education and development operations or projects; links training and development with other organizational units.

15. **Strategist:** Develops long-range plans for what the training and development structure, organization, direction, policies, programs, services and practices will be in order to accomplish the training and development mission.

Some of the proceeding list will not be appropriate to your efforts precisely, but at one time or the other you will probably work within a variation of these roles as you plan for and train others.

VARIED ROLES WITHIN A TRAINING

The competencies listed by ASTD give a view of what roles a trainer has in the broad sense of the job. The roles that concern most trainers, however, are those that must be orchestrated within the framework of the training itself.

As content needs change along with the needs of the audience, trainers must make an immediate decision as to how to address these shifts. When you see, for example, an entire audience demonstrate overt resistance when a particular subject or instruction is brought up, you must instantly decide how to counter and manage it. What should be your posture? Your demeanor? What strategy should you employ? How much control should you exert? Is "venting" useful or hurtful for the audience? What training techniques would most likely bring about the desired results? etc.

To equip yourself for these eventualities, give some thought to the different roles trainers are called upon to adopt within training sessions, including those offered here from the work of Yarbrough and Friedman in *Training Strategies From Start to Finish*.[10] (See the chart from their book, Figure 2-1, p. 36, at the end of this chapter.)

PLANNER

Planner: The trainer helps trainees by first doing the homework necessary to know what the group needs in content and relationship to the subject. What is to be taught? How will people respond to this? Is it a change of norms? If so, what needs to be done to remove obstacles and resistance? What are the common goals of the trainees and the organization? How can the trainer best help people focus on their commonalities and reduce conflict or friction? How can the trainer assist people in integration into existing systems?

In the planning role, the trainer works to remain neutral (not taking "sides"), draws on his/her honest listening skills and may wish to use small groups and team-building strategies to strengthen training plans.

COUNSELOR

Counselor-Catalyst: The trainer sees that trainees are set in dysfunctional habits and therefore needs to encourage them to become more positive and open to new ideas or methods. Someone once said "Many an open mind should be closed for repairs!" and often trainers run into folks who insist they are open-minded, when in fact, they are closed to change, deviation or new ideas.

When this occurs, examine the issue around which you are teaching...does it touch on a program that will replace or parallel one the resistant learner(s) have instituted or are managing? If so, you have run into a delicate area that is **symbolic** to those involved, and you will have to tread carefully. Assure the people or person that the new system does not reflect negatively on them . . . what they created or directed in the past was exactly what was needed at the time, and that contribution set the stage for the new growth, etc. etc. Understand that many people confuse their work and their worth - so suggesting a replacement or competitor to their work can translate into "I'm worth less".

When in this role of counselor, trainers needs to be sensitive and empathizing as they work to stimulate change that will help people focus on the needs of the clients or program.

CONSULTANT

Consultant: The trainer sees that people are jumping to conclusions before they have all the facts needed to map out appropriate action and responses. If this occurs entirely within the confines of the workshop you will have an easier time of patiently offering them more facts and guiding them to better decisions. If, as so often happens, they COME to the training with misinformation, you will have to work harder to help them "un-learn" incorrect data.

In this role, the trainer needs to exert patience — sometimes **incredible** patience — as they help trainees acquire the needed facts and nuances around a subject. It is helpful to use an economy of words and remain logical in relating facts to them. You may wish to overcome blocks to understanding, by not only laying out what the facts **are** but what they are **NOT**. Often people are making decisions based on false perceptions or assumptions that are totally incorrect.

An example of this would be a group being trained in a new computer system that is to be installed in the office. It is critical that the trainer understand the circumstances under which the original computer system was inaugurated several years ago . . . with no preparation of the staff or training for individuals that would have allowed for different skill levels.

With this background, it would be predictable that the trainees, recently told that a new system was to be installed, would assume that the same lack of support and training would occur again. Their response, based on this assumption, would of course be, NO WAY! (Remember Mazlow's statement that "refusal to learn is more deeply a refusal to do." Here's a classic example.)

It is up to the trainer to uncover this negative assumption, be patient in hearing frustrations stored up from the past experience (within limits) and present the facts logically and sequentially as to what steps the organization has planned to train individuals, provide on-going support, etc.

In helping such an audience "come around", the trainer uses consultation tools and skills to list concerns, have the group adaptively respond with ways to solve potential problems, and provide directive learning on what plans are already underway to help ease folks into the new system. At no time, however, will the trainer be able to project to the audience that they can reverse the decision to bring in new computer systems. (This demonstrates the balance the trainer must keep between trainee and organizational needs.)

Case methods, hands-on learning, small group problem solving etc. would be strong methods to use in such a training, provided the trainer keeps control and structures discussion. A "What's your gripe?" session with an audience of 75 people would not work and would probably end up in a shouting match!

INFORMANT

Informant/Resource Linker: While working in the consultant role, the trainer may have noted that trainees have a limited list of problem solving methods to handle situations. In this case, the trainer can share other options they might use in addressing challenges, concerns, etc.

To go back to the example of bringing in a new computer system, the group might center all their potential solutions around bringing someone in from the outside to educate, consult and coach them as they run into problems or questions. At this point you, a trainer, may suggest directly that they consider identifying someone already in their system that could be tapped as an in-house consultant; or you might prefer to have the <u>group</u> come to that same conclusion and therefore initiate a brainstorming process based on the challenge of "how can you get help if no one from the 'outside' could get to you?"

In the informant/resource role, the trainer stimulates participants to discover new resources and methods to meet challenges. Also, by the very nature of the trainer's broad experiences with many other people, groups and information, they can offer insight that participants would otherwise have no way of knowing.

Recently, when training leaders of nonprofit and volunteer groups, I have worked to keep them informed on national legislation pertaining to volunteer service and the financial loan credit that is attached to it. Most people I address know little or nothing about the legislation, let alone the ramifications the laws will have on their recruitment, management, record keeping or organizational efforts. Regardless of the subject matter I am training, I feel it is my responsibility to share this information. In so doing, I am switching into my role as informant and resource linker.

EXPERT

Advocate or Expert: In some situations, trainees cannot decide on the best course of action between 2 or 3 options that all seem to have merit. At this point they often turn to a trainer for advice and expertise. It is a sign of trust and a request for guidance that needs to be accepted by the trainer.

The same role will emerge when trainees need to be set on a specific course. In training management for instance, the trainer needs to lay out the step by step process of the functions of management in their correct sequence. It is a time to project themselves as the expert they are rather than to try to get the audience to figure out for themselves what the functions are or how they interrelate.

In this role, the trainer needs to be credible and persuasive, offering examples and solid information from themselves and other accepted experts. They will need to be an advocate for what is being taught, projecting a passionate belief in the principles and effectiveness of the subject. Persuasive lecture, case studies, role playing, etc. may all be used to get the message across.

COACH

Coach: When training requires that people learn a specific skill that they will have to use over and over again, the trainer slips into the role of coach. They demonstrate the skill, showing the trainee how the task is accomplished. They are methodical and use the same pattern over and over again. They avoid overuse of words and/or garble and reinforce the pattern in the same manner during each demonstration. They model the activity of learning and ask for feedback to insure that trainees are understanding what they are to do.

As trainer, you demonstrate the skill and help the audience practice the learning. Trainees are encouraged to ask questions to help them clarify the hows, whys and whats of the task before them.

FLEXIBILITY

These six roles — Planner, Counselor, Consultant, Informant, Expert and Coach — are all parts that you will need to be prepared to take on as you train people in any subject. Adult training obviously demands high skill levels in each, and the ability to switch to the role that is most appropriate to the learning goals, using great flexibility in order to accommodate the needs of the trainees <u>and</u> meet the training goals of the organization or client which asked you to do the training.

Rather than being manipulative, this flexibility is designed to ease learning for the variety of people and skill levels that confront trainers in any setting. Like the conductor of a great symphony, it demands an understanding of all the parts, a proficiency in specific instruments and a total grasp of how the whole is being played out.

The role of the trainer must never be underestimated. The good trainer is constantly increasing his or her repertoire of training skills and methods in order to meet changing needs of various audiences and subjects. Every training experiences is internally evaluated for what could have been done better, what worked well and what might have gone wrong. From this self-evaluation and buoyed by participants feedback, the trainer constantly works to improve future performances.

It's not easy, but it's worth it!

THE TRAINER'S ATTITUDE

Beyond the understanding of a trainer's various roles, the many directions they must think, what competencies they must have, how to plan and manage training and a total mastery of the subject matter — there is one more critical aspect to effective training. It is subtle, hard to calculate, difficult to teach and impossible to mandate.

I refer, of course, to the **attitude of the trainer.**

ADULT PERCEPTION

Let me begin with a simple statement: **Adult audiences are smart.**

They have been around longer than children, who are mandated to attend class and have no choice but to accept the teacher and what they have to say.

In the case of adults, even though some of them are forced to attend a training, they do not have to accept what is being said. They also have the courage of their convictions and are more than likely to challenge a trainer from the floor or complain to workshop coordinators if the training is below par.

CONTENT ESSENCE

If you ever do an analysis of complaints, you will find a distinct line drawn between content and relationships. If participants are unhappy with the content because it presents a concept or change they resist, they will voice their concerns in the workshop itself. They are upset with the essence of the content, even though it may have been presented very well (i.e.: a stated position on abortion/right to life/choice).

POOR TRAINING

If the essence of the subject is acceptable but the training itself is presented poorly, they will challenge the trainer from the floor and voice their disapproval even more loudly as they fill out their evaluations.

POOR ATTITUDE

It makes no difference if the content, subject and presentation are valid however, if the attitude of the trainer is perceived as condescending, arrogant, uncaring or in any other way negative. In such cases, participants will usually "attack" the trainer by voicing their displeasure during the workshop, personally criticize via the evaluations or make sure they speak to anyone scheduling trainers in the future to make their concerns known.

In the long run, having people perceive that a trainer has a bad attitude is far more damaging than having folks simply think the trainer came poorly prepared or had less than sterling training skills. The perception is that poor trainers can improve their skill levels, but those with poor attitudes probably won't change.

FOUR TRAINER HORRORS

Let me introduce you to some trainers we both might agree should go into some other line of work. Examine their attitudes:

Cary CONFRONTIST: She is a good trainer if you only look at her written materials or examples of her key points on a subject. Unfortunately, however, one of her personal goals is to see if she can rile up an audience by confronting people. Rather than healthy, positive confrontation, she loves to attack people personally. A graduate of the Morton Downey Jr. School of Communication, she measures her success in workshops by how many times people shouted at her, or how many attendees ended up in tears, rage or conniption fits. Her briefcase has notches on the handle for those people she made "loose their cool", and her lifetime goal is to have someone have a stroke in one of her workshops.

She loves to be obnoxious, twist people's words around, intentionally misconstrue what is being said and challenge people by personally attacking their integrity, values and intelligence. She keeps score and is bent on making sure she "wins" every confrontation.

Polly POMPOUS: Her mother told her she had an extremely high I.Q. and would probably go through life having to put up with people vastly inferior to her. She believed it. She chose training because of it. Lucky world.

This trainer has all the answers and if you ask her a question she can't answer she simply dismisses the asker with a "that's-just-too-stupid-to-answer!" wave of the hand. She worships daily at her full-length mirror, then grits her teeth for another training session with the peasants. When someone raises an idea or wants to share an example of the concept on the floor, she cuts them off, knowing it can't be valid. She employs the sit-still-while-I-instill" technique of training and finds ridiculous such things as brainstorming ("trainees are have no brains"), group discussion ("what could they possibly have to share?") or case studies ("invalid").

Her only "warmth" comes in the last 15 minutes of a session in which she hawks her brilliant and all-knowing books, videos, audios, encyclopedias and engraved stone tablets to the audience. She is generous, however, because attendees are only required to buy 3 of her items at $89.95 each, Visa and MasterCharge accepted.

Sammy SNIDE: Having earned his SPhD (Doctor of Snide Philosophy) from the Leona Helmsley School of Arrogance, he comes to a training career after many years in the investigation division of "Cheatum Insurance Co." Physically he would be rather non-descript, were it not for the permanent curl of his upper lip and his interesting inability to open his eyes wider than a slit.

He has chosen to specialize in training within the nonprofit sector because, as he wrote to his mother in New York, "I am wise to their tricks". He delivers his training in a constant monotone, because he knows the audience is a bunch of bleeding hearts and he doesn't want to play into their silly games. When asked a question, he avoids eye contact while shaking his head in disbelief at the stupidity expressed and, with a deep sigh, trys to "straighten them out" so he can go on to the next point.

He uses sarcasm to belittle attendees, holds the state record in "glowering" (wide-eyed division) at trainees challenging his singular opinions, and is a leader in the anti-flexibility movement. A first cousin to the executed Romanian dictator, he and Polly Pompous have been dating recently and were seen holding hands at a recent public hanging in Albania. Can wedding bells be far behind?

Subterranean SLICK: With 17 years experience selling used cars and "Rolex" watches on any given street corner in the Bronx, old Sub decided he was ready for the training game. With the blessing of his Uncle Harry (winner, for the 3rd year in a row of the model prisoner award at Sing-Sing), and his dear little Boopsie, an itinerant evangelist, he set out with flip chart, markers and his degree in adult education (obtained in just 8 easy payments), a fantastic résumé (a bonus for sending the first payment on time) and all the guile he could muster, to WOW audiences everywhere.

We have to give Sub his due...he's learned how to charm the feathers off a duck and tell a great story better than any flim-flam man on the East Coast. Audiences are in stitches for the first ten minutes of his presentation. They are amused for the next 10, then became anxious to have him get to the actual learning segment of his talk. By coffee break, Sub can sense something going awry as people began to boo him and he is grateful to spot a handy exit from the training room as attendees began to form a posse 10 minutes before his closing.

There was no substance to his training, he tried to mask this by breaking people into groups to discuss "whatever". His instructions were unclear and peppered with winks, smiles and little "funnies". The only handouts were Far Side cartoons and game tokens. When people confronted him and demanded he get down to the issue at hand, he bowed his head and suggested they all pray. (When challenged a second time, he tap danced.)

Last heard from, he was refusing to pay his 6th payment on his degree and planning to "do right" by Boopsie.

UNACCCEPTABLE ATTITUDES

Exaggerated? Of course, but in essence each example demonstrates attitudes that are not acceptable to the mature, thinking and experienced audiences out there who come to a training with an expectation and need for solid content, good training skills AND an attitude of respect. Being slick, snide, pompous or confrontational is **NOT** OK. It says that the goal of the trainer is aimed at themselves rather than the trainees or the information.

All smack of ego-mania and arrogance, two characteristics that, in the 90's, have soundly been rejected by individuals, groups and populations around the world. Ask followers of Jimmy Bakker and Gary Hart, the public in the Philippines, Panama, Romania, Poland, Russia, etc., investors in Wall Street, workers in the Helmsley hotels and voters in local park districts, school boards and municipal elections, and you'll find a pattern that rejects prima-donna, "I-am-above-the-rules" thinking.

What IS accepted . . . even demanded . . . in the way of trainer's attitudes is honesty, integrity, openness and caring.

HONESTY

Trainers need, first of all, to be honest. They need to project a validity and congruence that the audience can see and feel. No hype, no hoops and loops, no laser lights or bells or whistles . . . just open, "here-I-am" and "here's what I want to share" presentations.

I believe that having experience as a practitioner in what you are training is a major boost in having validity with an audience. I've sat through training as a program director where the trainer was offering his "wisdom" on recruiting and it was as plain as the nose on your face that he had never REALLY had to go out and recruit folks. He didn't know what it was like to have people turn him down, slip through his fingers, drop out or resist due to misinformation. He acted as though recruiting was no "big deal" if done correctly and could bring as many perfect people as needed to jobs if only we, the attendees, used his instruction.

INTEGRITY

Personal integrity is critical also, and must come across to an audience. Trainees need to trust the trainer so that they can, in turn, trust the instruction and information. Sharing war stories, experiences and even failures can help attendees sense a level of personal integrity that helps them accept the training.

Nothing is more important for you to attend to constantly than your personal reputation. Keep the quality of your training at the highest level possible. Upgrade your skills and information constantly so that you are sharing valuable insight in better and better ways. Try new techniques to add life to your efforts. If you create products, make sure they are the finest you can produce.

KEEP CURRENT

Check your assumptions and conclusions regarding what training is needed. Make sure you keep up to date with the changing faces of your audiences. Insure that you have allowed enough time to talk with people in your field, read the latest information and stay on the cutting edge. Don't just re-cycle old training, revitalize it.

AVOID POWER STRUGGLES

If, heaven forbid, you hear incorrect information being shared about you or what you offer, respond with correct information, but avoid power struggles at all costs (everyone loses in those). Avoid defensiveness, let the quality of your work speak for you. Grit your teeth and go on.

CARE

Care about your audience. Care about them as individuals trying to do the best job possible with the tools and time frames given them. Care that they be given information and tools to help ease their job and increase their effectiveness. Be patient and work with them until what you are saying makes sense to them and they can find a way to use it.

I believe that good training should put tools in trainees hands that they can use immediately, if not sooner! Make training practical, easy to use and dot all i's in the ink of common sense.

RESPECT

Respect the intelligence and dedication of the audience. If they are frustrated, allow them that feeling (feelings are facts, folks!) and help them move to diagnosing their frustration and finding ways to reduce or eliminate it.

Do not confuse caring about the audience with being loved by them. Sometimes you will have to say tough stuff . . . sometimes you will have to impose on them rules and methods that are distasteful. At times like this your goal cannot be winning a popularity contest, but doing the necessary work to equip them as best you can. Avoid having the attention shifted from the content to you as trainer. Idol worship is not healthy for anyone and leads to eventual "clay feet" reality.

Even when having to teach unpopular or resisted content, you can project concern and caring for them and their success. In so doing, you are again demonstrating your personal integrity, which is simply another facet of caring.

BE OPEN

Be open with your audience. If you don's know the answer to a question, ask the audience for assistance and admit you don't know. Don't hesitate to tell stories on yourself, how you learned a lesson the hard way or made a mistake. It simply tells people you are human, and gets across the important message that mistakes are not failures if they serve as learning.

PASSION

The last ingredient of a good attitude is one of my own personal preference: PASSION. I find that my training takes on a new dimension when I am training in a subject that evokes passion within myself.

I'm not referring to a theatrical training style of beating my chest or writhing on the floor . . . I'm talking about projecting a feeling of total commitment to what I am saying through congruent words and actions. I believe, for example, in the critical importance of people who work in care giving positions (directly or managerially) taking their own wellness as seriously as they do that of their clients and fellow-workers.

I am passionate about this. I can share personal experiences that demonstrate how I came to have this passion. I can become a soap-box orator on the subject given one attentive listener and 5 minutes of time! And I'm told it shows.

I urge you to examine potential subjects that you can teach and train in that afford you the joy of sharing a passion within you. In the process of that sharing, keep your own personal integrity, humanity, honesty, openness and caring as up-front and clearly obvious as any point of your content.

Care about the success of your audience, the quality of your content and the practicality of your training. Envision your audience as friends, colleagues and fellow travelers on this road called life who are deserving of your respect and admiration.

In so doing, you will not only be able to teach a lot, but you will be amazed at how much you will be enriched and able to learn!

TRAINER'S NO-no's!

Often in thinking of a role, it is as critical to address the subject from the angle of what is NOT acceptable, as it is from the perspective of what IS. This is true when defining a trainer's role with any audience.

A list of things to avoid would have to be personalized to each particular group and setting you might encounter (I'd avoid agricultural war stories to an audience made up of inner-city, East Coast participants, for example), but beyond the specific tailoring, there are several things you, as a trainer, will want to insure are NOT present in your training sessions or conferences:

1. Tunnel vision.

2. Canned presentations.

3. Reliance on old or out-dated information.

4. Assumptions regarding the audience.

5. Self-grandizement.

6. Telling negative stories about people or groups by name.

7. Baiting people or embarrassing them.

8. Jargon or unnecessarily complex wording.

9. A superior attitude.

TUNNEL VISION

Tunnel vision: You will want to avoid this style of thinking as a trainer because it is narrow, often bigoted, inflexible and frequently negative. It indicates that the trainer has chosen to view an issue or action in only one way and sets up confrontation and defensive behavior should anyone challenge this thinking. Rather than being a life long learner (one who constantly is learning new ideas, perspectives, etc.) it says that the trainer is closed to possibilities.

Much of adult learning is geared to having participants find creative options for their problems and work, and a trainer with tunnel vision is rarely able to lead people to such thinking.

Do not interpret this as meaning that trainers can hold no opinions . . . of course they can and do. However, you can state an opinion and invite others to express theirs, encouraging everyone to devise options of things that work best for them. Should a participant express an opinion that varies from yours, and it is possible that their opinion is fine for them, you have an opportunity to validate them. If, however, a participant makes a statement that your broader knowledge understands could be detrimental (ie: not having any job descriptions for workers), you have an obligation to confront the opinion (without attacking the person) and spell out the consequences of such actions. Remember that every "rule" has an exception!

CANNED PRESENTATIONS

Canned Presentations: If you train for any length of time on the same subjects, you will find yourself having to say the same things over and over again. You will be able to make each presentation fresh and unique if you avoid scripting your words. I once sat in on a training in which the trainer read her entire speech from a worn notebook. I had the distinct feeling that if I sat in the same workshop week after week I would have heard the same training, word for word.

A training session is not a stage play. It is not a time to memorize dialogue to be given each time you perform. There may be key phrases and technical instruction that remain the same, but the verbiage around them needs to be varied.

Work from key notes that show specific points you wish to make, but flesh them out with war stories and examples that are as up to date and relevant to the audience as possible.

When doing keynote speeches, be sure to personalize them to your listeners and keep them current. A fiery speech on the evils of domino communism in Europe would not be received well today in the light of the demise of that ideology in the early 1990's and would indicate to the audience that you were indeed, offering them a canned presentation.

OLD DATA

Reliance on old or out-dated information: The example used above regarding the keynote is classic of someone using out-dated information. In a training session it would become even more obvious if a trainer shares old data. Be sure to check your facts before presenting technical instructions. Know the latest about your client or the participants. Do not rely on your files that have been tucked away for 3 years on a subject or group . . . lots may have changed in the 3 years since you acquired the data and/or worked with the group. Get the facts!

ASSUMPTIONS

Assumptions: Watch out for this quiet killer. Assumptions . . . regarding the organization, audience, clients, product, service, climate, etc. etc. . . . have probably "done in" more trainers than airport hassles or old age ever could! Remind yourself daily and before every training session to NEVER assume. Be careful of attaching old tapes to new people. If the last time you worked with a particular national client they were focused on community development, you cannot presume that a chapter of the same group in a new location has the same agenda.

Guard against generalizations about an organization, region of the country, age of the audience, etc. Make sure you look at each new training as just that . . . NEW, and do your homework accordingly. Don't be afraid to ask dumb questions if you are unclear on something. Don't assume that the title of a group, project or any given set of participants clearly defines what it is they do.

I've sat through dozens of painful speeches and trainings as a member of a group of volunteer administrators where the speaker assumed the audience was made up of **volunteers.** As paid professionals who LEAD volunteer efforts, the assumption grated on our nerves and little was really heard of what the speaker was saying.

EGOMAINIA

Self grandizement: Sometimes, something sad happens to trainers who have accumulated a scrapbook and trophy case full of plaudits for their work and wisdom: Instead of putting them in their proper perspective (after all, a bronze trophy and a nickel still won't buy you a cup of coffee!), some trainers begin to believe their own press clippings and think they really do have **all** the answers. Such trainers begin to have a pattern of talking about how great **they** are, how **their** products will cure all ills and that **they** are the one true god of wisdom and knowledge.

Sadly, this often happens after they have indeed offered great contributions to a company, profession, field or group, but tends to obscure those contributions as they work to have people focus on **them** rather than the **learning** they present.

If all this sounds like a bad case of the "Founder Syndrome", you have labeled it correctly. Just as in the case of founders who feel pushed aside as new folks come into the picture, trainers who have redirected their focus from the content to their own personal relationship with audiences, can become obsessed with remaining in the spotlight or control. Continually watch to insure that you remain focused on the content you are delivering and the needs of the audience. If you deliver a good product and care about the learning, you will have all the plaudits you can ever handle! Besides, McDonalds still won't trade you a cup of coffee for your trophy!

NEGATIVES

Sharing Negatives: As a trainer or consultant, you will amass some experiences and information that are not exactly 100% flattering to the groups and individuals with whom you work. Because you are frequently called in to "fix" problems, you will acquire a growing list of war stories that demonstrate negative and unproductive actions, attitudes and consequences. It may be useful to use these stories in other trainings to share what can happen when things go wrong for a group, but NEVER name the group or individuals involved.

Consider yourself guided by the same principles as a doctor or lawyer in hearing about problems . . . **COMPLETE CONFIDENTIALITY**. If you do see a story as a positive example to use in teaching others, obscure it's facts while getting across it's learning principles. Avoid even hinting at it's name, clientele, actual product, location or any other potentially identifying characteristics. You can make your point without putting it, or yourself, in jeopardy.

EMBARRASSING PEOPLE

Baiting or Embarrassing People: I have often suspected that trainers who set audiences up for failure are really expressing a deep seated inferiority complex that demands that they put others "down" so they themselves, can be "on top".

Avoid anything that diminishes trainees personally. Even if a person comes up with a really peculiar statement that misses the mark by a mile, do not jump all over them, making personal attacks on their intelligence, integrity or propriety. Find a way to keep focused on the content of their statement and address it, possibly by drawing other opinions or statements from the audience that can ease people toward a more appropriate conclusion.

Do not "bait" people by drawing them toward a wrong conclusion only to pounce on them when they come to it, declaring them "stupid" or "illogical". (Leave that to such people as Morton Downey Jr.) Understand that when a trainer does embarrass or bait people, the rest of the audience becomes tense, looses it's confidence in the training and no longer trusts the speaker . . . all climate dimensions we need to avoid.

INAPPROPRIATE JARGON

Using Jargon: I have a rule of thumb that says "never use quarter words when nickel words will do." You might want to consider this as you train people, as it addresses the need to get the message across and eliminate obstacles to learning. You have many options of communication as you train . . . I believe that the simplest wording, most direct examples and clearest language are the route to take. Avoid jargon that your audience may not understand and words and phrases that may delight a creative writing professor but cause an audience to have to guess at what you are trying to say.

Start from the point of realizing that **a better word for communication is "interpretation",** everything you say will have to be stored in the brains of others through a filtering system known as interpretation. As individuals, we are all guided in this filtering by experiences, learnings and feelings from the past. With this as a backdrop, trainers need to insure that what they are saying will not be confused any more than necessary by unfamiliar, obscure or peculiar wordings.

As a trainer you have the option of saying: "Somewhere in midpoint of the instructional melee all the adults with physiological urgings will have the opportunity to partake, or imbibe, as the need may be, of repastorial delectables and assorted natural substances." . . . or . . . you can simply say: "At 10:30 we'll break for coffee and doughnuts."

SUPERIORITY

Superior Attitude: Here's the real no-no...one that says to the audience. "I'm smart . . . you're not," and immediately puts folks on the defensive. Believe me, just about the time you begin to think that you know <u>everything</u> about a subject, someone will come up with a totally new slant that makes you realize you really **don't** have all the answers. Such humbling experiences make us aware once again, that learning is a life long process rather than a rote recital of facts.

Approach training as a partnership with your audiences so that you can learn from one another by combining insights, experiences and learning. This helps you avoid any attitude of superiority.

In examining the role of a trainer, it is good to have a healthy perspective on what is and is **not** appropriate for a positive learning climate. Although audiences vary, basic rules of common respect, courtesy and appreciation prevail.

And if all else fails, just think of the Golden Rule and do unto trainees as you would have trainees do unto you!

COMMUNICATIONS: Getting Your Message Across

Very often HOW you say something is as critical as WHAT you say.

The best content falls on deaf ears if communication is garbled, poorly organized or presented in such a way that the audience is turned off.

To add to the challenge of communication, the attitudes, styles and patterns of the audience must be factored in to assess the best methods of getting your message across.

We know through testing that 45% of communication takes place without words and that only 35% of what is being said is understood.[11]

All this adds up to an incredible complexity that confronts trainers and consultants and must be a continual area of attention to insure that what was **heard** and what was **said** are as **close as possible.**

Notice I did not say "identical". After several decades in the training business, I've come to realize that we can never achieve perfect communication between two people, let alone the 100 or more we often find in seminars. I'm always bemused at people coming up to me and "quoting" something they were convinced they heard me say. Rarely is it 100% accurate, but if the underlying concept or thought is accurate, I don't correct them.

When it is too far off the mark, I do try to guide them gently to the real point, as I don't want to leave them with an incorrect direction. Interestingly enough, I frequently find they do not want to be corrected, because their interpretation was what they needed to hear, and my attempts to redirect them are rejected.

Elaine Yarbrough, an outstanding trainer in the area of communication and conflict, first helped me understand why being heard and understood is so difficult when she shared this basic clarification:

"INTERPRETATION is a better and more accurate word for COMMUNICATION".

When we understand that what is said is being sent by an individual who is placing interpretation on every word, to another who is receiving those words through their OWN set of interpretive filters, we become amazed that anything is understood between senders and receivers!

In her book *Communications: A Positive Message From You*, Trudy Seita tells us:

"The communications process is based on the theory that there is a sender, message, channel and a receiver. Both the sender and receiver are influenced by their culture, attitudes, values, knowledge of the subject of the message and even their environment. The message is the contents of the package being sent. It must have language which is understandable to the receiver, as well as be in a form that is acceptable to him".[12]

KEEP IT SIMPLE

As stated elsewhere, I am a strong advocate of keeping things as simple as possible. In dealing with organizations, I urge them to reduce processes, procedures, rules and regulations to a minimum for efficiency and creativity and to express those that remain in as few words as possible.

It's my belief that **we need to remove obstacles to understanding whenever possible.** This means that we find simple ways to tell people what we need them to know.

For training, this would mean:

1. State goal of the training . . . why you have called people together. (See Figure 2-2, p. 37, at the end of this chapter)

2. How much time the training will take.

3. What they will be able to do once they absorb the training.

4. Why the information is important to the goal of the organization and its' clients/consumers.

5. What concepts or issues will be covered in the training.

All of this information is best stated:

1. **Simply** . . . never use quarter words when nickel ones will do!

2. In **logical progression.**

3. With visual and participatory **reinforcements.**

4. **More than once,** using different communication methods.

5. With **feedback loops** to check audience understanding (asking questions; having trainees state learnings in own words; assigning task of adapting learning to a practical application, etc.)

If appropriate, assign sequential labels such as 1-2-3 or A-B-C or simply "first" "second", "third" etc. to help trainees keep things straight. **Be careful not to skip any part of the sequence or your audience will be confused.**

Do not try to tell people everything you know on a subject. Begin where your audience is and work up to where you need them to be without overwhelming or intimidating them.

Listen carefully and offer verbal feedback to assure you understood what is being said. Do not <u>over</u> respond to comments. Hear beyond the words to any hidden messages and keep eye contact with the speaker. Clarify what you feel unclear about. You may wish to check your listening skills by taking the quiz in Figure 2-3, p. 38, at the end of this chapter.

READ YOUR AUDIENCE

Read your audience carefully. With experience you will come to know if they have grasped the learning or are still confused. Go at their speed, reducing your content to the basic concepts if needed or adding much more information when desired and acceptable to the learners.

Avoid jargon that confuses people. Recently I received a proposal from a printing firm which wanted to get the contract to print our 25,000 product catalogs. The proposal consisted of 16 pages of printer jargon that was Greek to me!

When the firm's representative called to ask me if I'd read it, I told him I had but had gotten lost in his jargon. His response was that he had wanted me to know how thorough and professional his firm was and assumed I was familiar with printer's technical terms for inks, cuts, fonts, strips, etc.

I assured him that I know enough to express my needs but not enough to decipher what a "20/30/10 CSS/PMS overlay Pantone 6.2 vs 93.8 strip film laminate" was! (that's dark red, folks). The entire encounter, his subsequent defensiveness and not-so-subtle "how can you be so stupid" message turned me off. Need I say, he didn't get the contract?

He made two common communication errors...assumption and inappropriate goal . . . assuming I would understand intricate technical wording and forgetting that the goal of the proposal was to get my business, NOT to impress me with a complex presentation.

Avoid putting stumbling blocks between you and your listeners . . . how you say something is as important as what you say. Keep your eyes on the audience and read them carefully . . . they will signal their confusion or understanding directly. If you see participants so engrossed in the learning that they begin to verbally respond to questions you've put to the entire audience, you have a true indicator that they are absorbing the content.

BODY LANGUAGE & VOICE TONES

Trainers need to have an understanding of body language and voice tones from two different perspectives:

1. Their own.

2. That of others.

If a trainer says "I,m excited about what I have to share with you", but does so with a bored tone and a body stance that signals a lack of enthusiasm (slouching at the podium, leaning chin on hand, eyes half open, no eye contact with audience, etc.) very few adults will believe them.

CONGRUENCY

The problem is that the words do not match what the body is saying . . . The trainer is incongruent and can therefore have his/her statement rejected.

For a trainer to be CONGRUENT, words, body language and voice tone all need to be aligned.

"I believe in this!" along with direct eye contact, fervent expression and confident, strong voice tone will feel genuine.

"I believe in this . . ." accompanied by an impartial, weak voice tone, stiff body posture, and no eye contact, is suspect.

In assessing the true message you are getting from others, look for clues within them of their own congruency. Do words, postures, body language, voice tones etc. match? Do they help you believe what is being said? Do they all point to the same conclusion?

DIAGNOSING INCONGRUENCY

When people are incongruent, watch closely for characteristics that indicate any of the following four communication styles:

1. BLAMING:
   A. Words: accusatory or condescending ("My boss is stupid").
   B. Goal: to find someone to blame besides themselves ("I can't learn this junk; you talk too fast.").
   C. Body: use of finger pointing, loud voice tone, interrupting, overpowering, stomping feet, slapping desk, standing up and over others, etc.
   D. Feelings inside: threatened, lonely, unsuccessful, diminished.

2. PLACATING:
   A. Words: Agreeing constantly, accommodating, shifting opinions to please others, apologizing, offering profuse compliments.
   B. Goal: to be liked and accepted.
   C. Body: helpless, weak voice tone, retreating, slouching, arms in protective wrap around body, hands may be put in front of mouth or eyes, etc.
   D. Feelings inside: weak, worthless, stupid, unliked, unaccepted, etc.

3. COMPUTING:
   A. Words: ultra reasonable, diagnostic.
   B. Goal: "Don't attack me."
   C. Body: expressionless, rigidly calm, stiff, closed arm position often clutching on to elbows tightly, "uptight" voice tone, etc.
   D. Feelings inside: fragile, vulnerable, etc.

4. DISTRACTING
   A. Words: irrelevant, off the point, distancing.
   B. Goal: avoid the truth or conclusion with which they disagree.
   C. Body: angular, disjointed, hyperactive or distractive, high choking voice tone, stammer.
   D. Feeling inside: frantic, alone, rejected, etc.[13]

The common denominator for all of the four styles presented is **ANXIETY & FEAR.** Each person is frightened and personally anxious. It is up to the trainer/consultant to diagnose the fears and work to reduce or eliminate them so that they do not continue to produce inappropriate behavior and blocks to learning.

Keep in mind as you read this section, that I am sharing CLUES to what is really going on inside a person, not necessarily hard and fast facts.

If a person coughs in the middle of a sentence, many people believe it indicates lying, but in actuality they might just have to cough! Shifting from foot to foot may mean a person is uncomfortable with what they are saying OR it might mean their foot went to sleep! Avoid jumping to conclusions — as someone once said "A little knowledge <u>are</u> a dangerous thing!"

OPEN & CLOSED COMMUNICATION

Body language falls under two headings: **Open** and **Closed.** As you work with audiences or individuals, note their characteristics. If the person is open, they will be more receptive to what you are saying than if they are closed. If you do find them closed, you may wish to try to get to the bottom of this reaction. Are they fearful? Are they skeptical? Are they not trusting you or what you are saying? Are they bringing past "tapes" and experiences to the new information you are sharing?

Look for clues that tell you if they are open or closed and when they switch from one position to the other.

When people are open they tend to:

1. Seek and keep eye contact.

2. Lean forward.

3. Keep hands stretched toward you with palms up when seated.

4. Smile naturally.

5. Sit or stand relaxed.

When people are closed, they tend to:

1. Avoid eye contact.

2. Lean back.

3. Keep legs tucked under chair when seated.

4. Fold arms across chest.

5. Stay rigid.

6. Clench jaw.

THE CHALLENGE OF COMMUNICATION

In attempting to communicate ideas, concepts, instructions or general learning, keep in mind that the success in this challenge lies in your ability to interpret the audience and project your messages clearly and congruently. You must cultivate a mind set that is as open as possible and reduce your own prejudicial interpretations that might hinder other people's learning.

Communication has to be the most inexact science in the world, but we as trainers must depend on it as our main tool, and find ways to make our product of information travel as directly as possible between ourselves as senders and our trainees as receivers.

Say it simply.
Care about your audience's learning and comfort.
Show it.

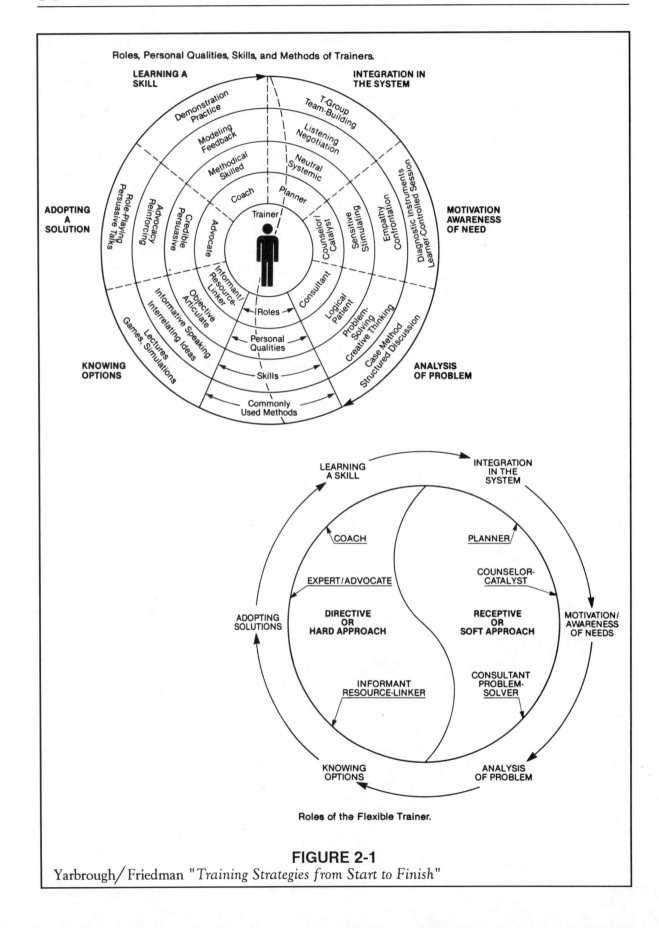

Roles, Personal Qualities, Skills, and Methods of Trainers.

Roles of the Flexible Trainer.

FIGURE 2-1

Yarbrough/Friedman "*Training Strategies from Start to Finish*"

IDENTIFY YOUR GOALS

Before asking "**How** do I train people?" you might first clarify your objectives.

Below is a list of some answers to the question "**Why** am I training these people?"

☐ to impart knowledge.
☐ to impart skills.
☐ to modify attitudes.
☐ to help them select a task.
☐ to tell them what they will be doing.
☐ to influence how they will do their work.
☐ to enable them to identify with the organization.
☐ to help them adapt to change.
☐ to increase their self-confidence.
☐ to respond to their needs.
☐ to tell them how to do the job.
☐ to offer them a chance to suggest new ideas or options.
☐ to accord them status.
☐ to enable them to recognize their potential.

Choose which goals are the most important to you, and then plan your training session accordingly. Select the method and content material which will best accomplish your aim.

FIGURE 2-2

A CHECKLIST FOR IMPROVED LISTENING...

(How many of these do you practice?)

☐ When I give an instruction, do I obtain feedback to assure I am understood?

☐ Do I give my listeners cues to know when "to tune me in"?

☐ Do I understand that I not only have the right to influence others but they also have the right to influence me?

☐ Do I know my bias and prejudices so that they do not unduly filter out certain messages?

☐ Do I understand that people "speak" through a myriad of non-verbal ways, that I must "hear" this communication too?

☐ If I were listener, would I listen to myself?

☐ Do I understand that when a person feels he is being understood, he tends to be less aggressive and less defensive?

☐ Do I understand that being a good listener does not mean I must believe what I am hearing or subscribe to the values of the speaker?

☐ Do I understand that I am learning little when I am talking?

☐ Do I try not to over-respond to emotionally charged words?

☐ When I disagree with something, or find something exciting, do I take pains to listen carefully?

☐ If I am having trouble being understood, do I understand that the burden is on me to try to understand the other fellow?

☐ Do I know when I may be intimidating listeners though threatening behavior?

☐ Can I tell when there is a hostile, emotionally charged atmosphere?

☐ Do I consider the person involved as well as the situation?

☐ Have I taken pains to understand this person?

☐ Do I listen for what is *not* being said?

☐ Do I listen for telling tone as well as for words?

☐ Do I also *look* as if I am list

Looking Into Leadership/Executive Library Leslie E. This

FIGURE 2-3

CHAPTER 3

The Audience of Adult Learners

In looking at the overall picture of training, we must spend some time examining the role of the audience. Whether the training is geared for one person doing a particular job or 400 learning a new procedure, the trainer needs to accumulate as much insight as possible into how adults learn, how to assist them in their learning process and how to eliminate blocks to learning.

It would be great if there were just one simple list of a few things trainers would need to learn that would tell them all about adult learning, but, because individuals are unique, we must look at adult learning from several different angles. To add to the complexity of this subject, you, as a trainer, must never close the book on this topic, because each time you teach a person or group, you will add to your own body of knowledge as to how adults learn most effectively.

In her writings, Harriet Naylor states: "Unless training does reach the level of learning which will make a difference in behavior and influence decision making, the effect of the teaching effort will be quite transitory."[14]

Naylor goes on to say, "Learning which will change our ways, our habits and point of view, must touch us deeply."[15]

If change and different behavior are indeed our goal as we train others, we must look at how people learn from many different perspectives, and then keep on learning through our own first hand experiences in teaching others.

ADULT LEARNING STYLES

A place to begin understanding adult learners is in examining three basic ways people take in information and that each has its own set of filters through which all input must pass. It is fascinating to see two different people interpret the SAME FACTS very differently.

INTERPRETATION

This again points up the challenge of communication, as it is really an exercise in interpretation, with various receptors (your audience) interpreting the same information differently. You can say to one person, "I'm so pleased to see you," and they will smile warmly and respond, "Thank you, I'm delighted you're here too."

You can then say the exact same thing, with the same voice tone and body language to the next person and their response can be, "What do you mean you are 'pleased to see me', did you think I wouldn't show up?" Same initiating statement, two different responses . . . one positive, one defensive. Why?. . . because as individuals, we carry unique sets of life experiences, attitudes and learnings, and therefore can come up with distinctly different interpretations and responses to the same input.

In this example, the first person may have gotten up in the morning feeling very rested, came to work excited about the agenda for the day and eager to learn. The second may have been up all night trying to clean out a flooded basement, drove to work in a rush, grinding his teeth all the way over the issue of being denied a raise last week, and angry that one more day was to be "wasted" on outside training that pulls him away from his overloaded desk. The baggage each person was carrying was reflected in their individual responses to the same, friendly statement, "I'm so pleased to see you."

This "baggage" or "filter system" is attached to the ways in which adults learn:

1. Auditorially.

2. Visually.

3. Hands on.

The way in which a person prefers to receive information determines the best and most effective route to get learning points across.

AUDITORY LEARNERS

The AUDITORY LEARNER learns by hearing the trainer's key points, and reinforces this learning by offering spoken feedback either to the trainer or other learners. They tend to best recall what they have **heard.**

VISUAL LEARNERS

The VISUAL LEARNER learns through seeing key points written down, offered on an overhead projector or some type of visual communication (film, charts, graphs, etc.). They tend to recall what they have read or **seen.** They take particular interest in role playing or films of actual work that depict what they will have to do.

HANDS-ON LEARNERS

The HANDS-ON LEARNER learns through applying spoken or written theory to actual practice. Since small group discussions often take theoretical learning into the practical state, they respond to such exercises. Like the visual learner, they gain a great deal of insight from viewing role plays or films of actual work experiences and like to reinforce this learning by experimenting with it **first hand.** Their best method of learning comes, of course, by being trained "on the job."

A MIX OF LEARNINGS

In training adults, the most effective method, which actually employs all three learning stances, is to have the trainee walk through the work with their supervisor or predecessor. It gives them first hand knowledge of the work that needs to be done, offers opportunities to ask questions and reinforces what they might have read about the work. If you are unable to offer this option in training, you can set up practice sessions to allow people to experience a simulation of the skill they are being taught.

As you train, mix your learning style and tools between auditory, visual and hands-on experiences in order to capture all of your audience. Be prepared that many in your audience will understand the concept or skill you are teaching when they first **hear** you explain it. A second group will not "get it" until you add a visual such as an overhead, a handout or written information on the flip chart. The third and last group will not really integrate the learning until they get to practice its application, either in the workshop setting or back on the job. (And by this time, the auditory learner who "got it" when you first said it, is getting restless and wishes you would get on with the training!)

If, in training, you have offered only auditory training (the most frequently used) and see a majority of puzzled faces in the audience, dip into your bag of tricks for some hands on and visual reinforcements . . . that should help your trainees in their learning experience!

ADULT LEARNING PRINCIPLES

Adults Learn Differently Than Kids!

Most of the learning we think of even as adults is actually the teaching we received as children. We remember having to sit still and keep quiet in most classes as we listened to teachers tell us what they said we needed to know.

By high school, we began to wonder why we might ever need to know the square root of 158, the distance to Mars or the names of all the defeated Presidential candidates since George Washington's election, but we did understand that doing so meant the difference between graduating or being on the 6 year plan!

By college we had formed strong opinions on what we needed to learn, but still had to sit through, and pass, some graduation requirements a committee had decided on after hibernating in a cave for 11 months. Art majors had to pass meteorology, chemistry majors suffered through art, pre-med grimaced while taking modern dance and cinematography majors made jokes (outside of class of course) about how they might work advanced calculus into a future award winning film.

Classes recalled most warmly by adults tend to be those in which the teacher involved them in the learning and respected what they, the student, could bring to the lessons. For the most part, however, the role of the student was one of "sit still while I instill" and learning was for many, something that had to be endured if it was outside the sphere of chosen course work.

I doubt that anyone will go into shock when I say that adults learn differently than children. (What is interesting, is that we are now coming to understand that the learning demands of adults are frequently found to be most effective when used with children, but that's food for another book.)

ADULT VS. CHILD LEARNERS

Malcolm Knowles,[16] one of our great teachers on adult learning, shares several ways in which adults differ from children in their learning patterns and needs:

1. **Adults have more experience:** They have more examples and parallels to draw upon as they learn. Be sure to bring them into the learning by offering them the opportunity to share past experiences pertinent to the training. Often they can give a concrete example of a principle the trainer is speaking about and thereby clarify it to themselves and the training group.

2. **Adults are ready to learn:** Kids rarely see the value of what is being taught unless it is something that is a desired skill, such as riding a bike or batting a ball. Because of this, a great part of the teacher's job is in getting and keeping them interested. Except in the instances where training is mandated and seen as threatening to the learner (the great exception to the norm, by the way), adults are eager to learn and therefore expect the teacher to teach them well.

3. **Adults want the training NOW!:** Children tend to feel that what they are being taught is something that they may or can use at some point in the distant future ("When I grow up and am an astronaut"). Adults, on the other hand, want the information to be presented in such a way that they can use it immediately. They expect to get up from the training table either able to do old things better or new things well.

4. **Adults want learning to be practical:** They have a common demand, too frequently unheard by trainers: "CUT TO THE CHASE!" . . . "GIVE ME BARE BONES!" . . . "MAKE SENSE!" Don't overload trainees with mucky theory that can be debated for the next 6 years. Making the training more and more complex without giving participants examples and exercises for practical application may turn your audience into an angry mob. When theory needs to be presented, do so in the simplest words possible (never use quarter words when nickel words will do), reinforce the concept with hands-on and visual learning techniques; help folks apply the theory to real life experiences and ask a lot of questions to make sure they understand what is being said. Do not try to impress the audience with everything you know on a subject . . . simply offer information that the audience needs and can use in the most practical sense. View information as a tool to use, not a stagnant possession.

5. **Adults have a clearer self concept:** They know what skills they have, what they need and what things they do or don't do well. Listen to them, they are the experts on themselves for the most part. Let them tell you what they need to know beyond what basic information you give them.

   If they say they need to read more about the subject you are teaching, offer them suggested references. If they ask you to go over a particular point once again, do so. They are telling you it's not as clear as they would like it to be in their mind.

Adults are more mature than children and have gained self confidence, so they will be more outspoken in their demands on you. That's great and offers you opportunities to provide requested background information and a variety of teaching methods to assist the transfer of learning from theory to reality for them.

Occasionally you will run into a person who has a poor self-image and underestimates their own skill level. When you identify this, you will need to bring them along gently, first going where they say they are and helping them discover the richness in themselves that they had not seen before.

Never embarrass such people in front of a group to try to bring out their talents. A teacher such as Robin Williams played in the movie, *Dead Poets Society* can try that, first because it's fiction and secondly because in real life a teacher has about 200 days of interaction with the student to insure the technique did not do great harm. A trainer does not have such a luxury and needs to avoid making a participant fell embarrassed.

Adults do indeed learn differently than children and can therefore bring a richness and depth to training that, when tapped and respected, can add immense dimension to the learning experience.

ADULT NEEDS AND MOTIVATIONS

It is important to take a step back and look at adults from the angle of behavioral science by understanding what motivations and needs they bring to training sessions.

Abraham Maslow gave us his famous *Hierarchy of Needs* which categorizes five basic needs that people have: Physiological (food, water, etc.), Safety (free from danger), Social (relationships), Esteem (recognition for worth), and Self-Actualization (need to be the best they can be). Let's take a look at each and see how they help us understand potential trainee's needs:

PHYSIOLOGICAL

This need should be quite apparent! If you have ever sat in an uncomfortable chair, with no opportunity to get up and stretch for more than an hour, you can clearly articulate your basic need. When training, offer attendees the options of moving around, getting some refreshments, using the restrooms, interacting with others, etc. When such needs are unmet, they become the dominant thinking and consequently block all that great information you are trying to impart! A rule of thumb: as the age of the audience goes up, their ability to withstand physical discomfort goes down! Work to break your training into smaller time bits, so that folks can meet their physical comfort needs.

SAFETY

Obviously, people in any training setting need to feel physically secure . . . offering a training setting in a dangerous neighborhood will probably prevent some people from attending and those that do may constantly be thinking about when they will be leaving and how safe the parking lot will be. In planning your workshops, keep the factors of physical safety in mind and choose locations in accordance with the need of participants and faculty to avoid any harm. If you must be in a specific location (a hospital in a high crime area, for example), take necessary measures to insure everyone's safety. This might include timing for the training, special, secure parking arrangements and even escorts to and from the building.

In your publicity for the training, be sure to list all these measures and invite any people still concerned to call you or someone you designate to discuss the safety. Stress SAFETY in your communications, by the way, not the DANGER.

In looking at safety needs of trainees, we must also examine it from the intangible perspective . . . the feeling of safety within the training. From this angle, the participant needs to feel he or she is not going to be attacked verbally by the trainer or group when expressing opinions or asking questions.

Audiences need to feel enough trust in the climate and norms of the group that they can risk creative thinking, asking "dumb" questions, offering feedback and generally being able to interact with the training in positive ways. They need to feel secure and safe enough to be open in their communications. The pattern for this trust is established, managed and communicated by the trainer, who sets the norm either by example, by direct statement or both.

It is critical for adults to feel safe in a training so that they can be free to fully participate in the transfer of learning that must be accomplished for true effectiveness.

SOCIAL

Keep in mind that there are two faces to training. . .the content and the relationships. Adults have needs at varying levels of relationships, and it is up to the trainer to establish a climate that accepts these levels.

Some folks have a need to interact dramatically with other participants; others need to interact with the trainer, still others need to minimize relationships with others in attendance and instead, confine themselves to relating to the material and only those other participants from their particular setting or discipline.

It is safe to say that everyone will come to a training with some need to relate to others. Do not confine your interpretation of this social need only to such things as fun and parties . . . it is more deeply a need to connect and inter-relate to other people, whether they are in the training itself or back on the job.

ESTEEM

This basic need refers to the quest for respect and recognition from others. In training sessions, you as trainer will set the climate that affirms people. Find ways to offer opportunities for participants to share examples that clarify concepts and help others learn. Spotlight outstanding efforts of trainees, working to find a way to honor as many people as possible during the session. Avoid anything that might diminish, tarnish or place blame on anyone present. Do not "bad-mouth" any group or individual. Do not name participants who stand as a negative example.

In esteeming people, be honest and sincere. Flattery given when it is not deserved is a red flag to people and frequently interpreted as the mark of an insincere and untrustworthy person. From that point forward even deserved praise from the same person is looked at skeptically. If you have ever been involved in a group setting where the leader gushes over everyone simply for having shown up, you know how uncomfortable such fake "esteem" can feel.

SELF ACTUALIZATION

This need reflects people's desire to do and be the best they can. . .an artist strives for the perfect painting; the writer for the great book; the manager for the smoothest operations; the doctor for the cured patient. People want to be successful and they want the trainer to help them achieve this success.

In the training itself, they want clear instructions that allow them to come to correct conclusions, complete exercises successfully, interact appropriately and give the best possible answers to tough questions.

Beyond the training, they want to use learned skills and insights to help them "do" things better or "be" better as they go about their work, interacting with family, friends and colleagues. Learning is a tool to be put to use immediately and forever, or until a better tool comes along. Insight, "ah-ha's" and connections are highly valued. Trainers are looked upon as partners in learning and sharing knowledge is prized.

UNMET NEEDS MOTIVATE

These five categories of need proceed in a pattern that Maslow tells us must be satisfied at a lower level before the needs at a higher level can be addressed. People will not remain in a self-actualization stance if they have physiological needs for a stretch break and nourishment. Esteem needs won't predominate if a person is worried about their physical safety at the end of the session, etc.

Maslow says that an "unmet need motivates; a met need does not," meaning that if a person has a full stomach, offering them the reward of more food will not stimulate them to action. In modern days, if a person feels esteemed and has a full social calendar indicating numerous opportunities to relate to people they value, offering them a new job based on a chance to earn more awards or make new friends, will probably not turn them on.

Maslow also tells us that we gravitate to the lowest level of need on his hierarchy. A person solidly motivated by needs of self-actualization will abandon any concern with this need level when they become ill and have deep concerns about their health. A person with deep esteem needs will drop to a safety level when hearing that her company has just been sold to an Arab oil sheik who plans to fire 50% of the staff.

In training adults, keep in mind their psychological needs, recognizing through clues they give you, as to their own particular level. Understand also, that there are certain norms you, as the trainer, can set and control within the training, that provide everyone's ongoing needs for physical comfort, security, interaction, respect and effective learning. In so doing, you are setting the stage for "learning which will change our ways, our habits and point of view. . .by touching us deeply."[17]

READINESS TO LEARN

One of the major learnings a teacher of children must acquire is how to bring them to the point of being ready to learn.

For adults who choose training voluntarily, the trainer is given the gift of an audience anxious to acquire information. The main concern the trainer must then address is what expectations did they bring with them?

THEORY OF EXPECTANCY

Behaviorist Victor Vroom offers us his *Theory of Expectancy* which simply says that when reality does not live up to expectations, people feel cheated, upset and disillusioned. It is critical, therefore, to uncover expectations at the start of the training.

Asking for needs and desired outcomes as you start the session is only one of many techniques to begin this process. Whatever you feel is appropriate for your audience should be your guide. Do all you can to have trainees tell you their expectations. If they are unrealistic, say so and involve them in thinking of ways to meet their expectations. NEVER PROMISE WHAT YOU CAN'T DELIVER, however!

LEVELS OF LEARNING

For people who do not come voluntarily or those who come only out of curiosity, you will need to consider the natural progression of learning levels offered by several writers. The same levels will need to be understood when dealing with people who require training in new techniques, processes, methods or skill building.

Walt Disney, one of this centuries most creative managers, offers his levels of learning:

Level 1: Unconscious Incompetence — This comes before a person even understands that training is needed — a "dumb and don't know it" position. Adults can find themselves in a place of not even realizing what they don't know or need to know — they can't find **answers** because they don't even know the **questions**.

The trainer's job at this point is to motivate people to want to learn — usually by helping them envision the goal of the training and what can be achieved once they are trained.

Level 2: Conscious Incompetence — This occurs when adults realize all their questions and how much they don't know. It can be a time of feeling overwhelmed at how much there is to learn and sometimes even a conviction that they are not going to be able to grasp everything required. They are not competent and they know it.

At this point, the trainer needs to become an affirming partner that assures trainees the subject can be learned and the learner can be successful.

Level 3: Conscious Competence — This comes as the trainee transfers learning into successful action and gains confidence that they can indeed do the work etc. They are competent and they know it.

The trainer's role is simply one of standing by for any requested additional assistance. This will occur to some extent if you are an in-house trainer with daily contact with trainees and often takes the pattern of coaching or consulting rather than actual training. If you interact with training audiences as an independent or outside trainer, it will happen less frequently.

Level 4: Unconscious Competence is the level many people come to after they have done something for a great length of time and begin to do them by rote. It's the "rut" stage. Some people dislike it because it no longer stimulates them — they simply do the work to get it done in the same pattern they have developed. It is actually a dangerous time, especially if their work includes machinery or the need for critical accuracy if they begin to let their mind drift while doing the required tasks.

If you are an in-house trainer or a consultant/trainer called in to evaluate an organization, you can try to spot such people and suggest that they be given new challenges for learning — returning them to Disney's first two levels of learning.

LAYERS OF LEARNING

In Naylor's book,[18] she offers six layers of learning that focus on information and the relationship the potential learner has to information. The six levels are:

1. **Unawareness.** Couldn't care less or haven't noticed.

2. **Awareness.** Notice, but wonder if it's true, valid, needed, etc.

3. **Interest.** Think this may turn out to be important.

4. **Acceptance.** Tested against experience or validators and it seems to be true.

5. **Conviction.** This is not only important for me, but for others.

6. **Commitment.** This is of great importance to me and determines how I feel and will react. I am passionate about it.

It is up to the trainer — whether they are in front of an audience they may only meet once or a trainer who works continually with many of the same people and coaches them on a regular basis — to recognize and bring people through the levels of learning and acceptance of information.

Recognize where people are and bring them along to the highest possible level that will allow them to feel competent and confident to do the required tasks. When dealing with multiple trainees simultaneously, such as in a workshop, you will have to juggle the different levels of various trainees to meet the needs of the group as a whole and the session's training objectives.

CHAPTER 4

EFFECTIVE TRAINING: FORMATS, METHODS AND CLIMATE

Like people, all workshops are unique, with different personalities, norms, climates, etc. however, there are characteristics we can track that seem to be present in one form or the other in effective workshops with adults.

Effective workshops seem to:

1. Involve participants and tap their experiences.

2. Allow participants to translate past experiences into new learning.

3. Be responsive to audience needs physically, emotionally and mentally.

4. Help participants build self confidence.

5. Raise people up rather than putting any one down. . .they reinforce positively.

6. Solve problems or rise to challenges the participants have in real life.

7. Allow enough time for people to integrate and translate information.

8. Allow time for direct application and are practical in their approach.

9. Present and assist in selection of options, promoting coping skills.

10. Define parameters around problems. . .what they are and are not.

11. Provide a safe environment to try new ideas and make first steps toward change.

12. Present information in varied ways.

13. Have breathing spaces between intense demands.

14. Encourage creativity and respect diversity.

15. Be aimed for the success of the participant.

16. Be fun and easy to take. . .comfortable.

17. Be respectful of cultural differences.

18. Be framed in common sense and flexibility.

19. Be led (rather than dogmatically controlled) by a well prepared, caring and knowledgeable trainer who spells out objectives and purpose, sees to smooth logistics, provides appropriate direction, processing, facilitation and information within a realistic schedule, using varied techniques for interaction.

WHEW!!!

As you work toward creating and presenting the best possible training, you will want to include as many items on this list as are reasonable. Do not, however, expect to include all of them, as different settings demand different responses to meet the needs of the trainees and the sponsoring organization.

To insure the best training, the trainer needs to be able to draw on a wealth of skills and understanding of a variety of formats and methods, plus a thorough knowledge of appropriate learning climates.

FORMATS OF TRAINING

In the formalized arena, training can come in several formats including orientation, skill building, coaching, consulting and general information. These can be categorized as "pre-job" and "on-the-job" training.

Learning methods, which are examined in the next section of this book, can be used to present the information within each variety. It is up to the trainer, in concert with the organization sponsoring the training, to select the best format to support the kind of training to be required.

<u>Who</u> offers the training is a critical piece of the perception of newcomers as to the importance the organization places in training. Naylor says "new people will estimate the value an organization puts on training by the status of the trainers, and will be strongly influenced by the attitudes displayed."[19]

Carefully select the trainers and the format to match the needs and perceptions of the audience so that trainees understand clearly the importance you place on training.

PRE-JOB TRAINING

ORIENTATION

In their book *Essential Volunteer Management*, authors Steve McCurley and Rick Lynch define orientation for volunteers coming into a new program, but because an orientation for anyone, volunteer or not, is the same, we can use it here:

> *"Orientation is the process of making people understand and feel comfortable with the workings of an agency. It is designed to provide them with background and practical information that they will use to relate what they are doing within the overall functions of the agency and to better understand how they can contribute to the purpose of the agency."[20]*

The American Heritage Dictionary[21] defines orientation as:

> *"A setting to familiarize with or adjust to a situation; to align or position with respect to a specific direction."*

As you can see from these definitions, an orientation has several purposes:

1. Provide information to acquaint people with the organization, agency or program and it's purpose or goal.

2. Help people understand where they fit into the process of making this goal or purpose happen.

3. To familiarize people with the organization so that they feel comfortable with its' workings.

4. Give people information they can use to relate or bond with the organization and its purpose.

5. Help people see how they can contribute productively.

Please note that some of these purposes deal with the work they will be DOING, others with how they FEEL about the organization and still another on their understanding of the purpose, goal or VISION of the organization.

Too frequently, orientations focus only on reciting facts and figures, history or the physical layout of an agency or group while the "softer" information relating to climate, feelings of security, bonding, and the purpose for being are skimmed over or omitted completely.

THERE IS NO MORE CRITICAL LEARNING FOR NEW RECRUITS THAN AN UNDERSTANDING OF WHAT THE PURPOSE OF AN ORGANIZATION OR EFFORT IS. On this foundation of understanding all additional information will be built, and if it is faulty or non existent, nothing else can be sound!

For example, if a new recruit comes into an organization such as Meals On Wheels and thinks, erroneously, that the purpose of the group is simply to feed people food, she/he may work to create "super efficiency" by designing a plan for clients to drive through a local bank and pick up 30 frozen dinners to be used each day for a month.

Though a great study in time efficiency, it fails the REAL mission of Meals On Wheels which is to provide regular, personal interaction between clients and volunteers along with nutritionally balanced meals. It would feed their bodies but not their souls. (It also shows a lack of understanding of the ability of most clients to drive to a site and physically carry and store 30 frozen dinners.)

Imagine what could happen in a commercial firm if a new recruit didn't understand the company mission. A person who thinks the goal is to get rid of as many widgets as possible versus solving customer's problems and developing long term relationships would approach their job very differently!

ORIENTATION AGENDA

An agenda for an orientation might look like this:

1. Welcome.

2. Describe the purpose and vision of the organization (program, etc.).

3. Offer history from first vision to present day activities.

4. Describe clientele and what the goal is in interacting with them.

5. Sketch out organizational chart, complete with names and chief responsibilities of each and how they interact . . . indicate where the new recruit's job fits.

6. Timelines showing major events and activities.

7. Introduction to facilities, equipment, products, promotions, etc.

8. Description of procedures, guidelines, rules, benefits, etc.

9. Questions from audience.

10. Description of further training, interaction, support, etc.

11. Reminder of vision of organization and how audience fits into the whole mission plus the importance of their contribution to its success.

You will find other items to add to the agenda for the orientation in accordance with specific needs of both the trainees and the organization. As you design it, consider that it should answer the following questions that trainees will have (though they may not express them openly):

"What should I know about this organization and location
    to best understand it?"
"Who should I know about?
"Where it is going? What's the goal?"
"Why do you want me? What can I contribute?"
"How will I be supported?"
"What advancement possibilities might exist for me?"

You may wish to involve other staff or peers of the trainees so they can meet the recruits and provide overviews of their efforts. Remember that the information offered in an orientation is more general than a training, which is geared more toward specifics of a position.

FORMAL TRAINING

This is offered for the purpose of preparing people for a specific job. The learning falls into three categories:

1. Responsibilities.

2. Job actions.

3. Roles and relationships.

For **responsibilities**, the trainer gives an overview of specific duties of the recruit, offering increasing details of what is expected and what the goal is of the effort.

In training related to **actions**, it is important to outline "do's" and "don'ts" plus offering examples of situations that allow participants to choose responses and have the benefit of the trainer's guidance toward appropriate conclusions. The trainer clearly details the functions of the job both verbally and in writing and has the trainee either repeat it orally or practice the skill directly for the trainer to observe and evaluate.

In offering **relational** information, specific guidance is offered as to how departments, programs and individuals interrelate and work together for efficiency and success. It also offers specific insight into the trainee's roles and how they "fit" into the overall organization's efforts.

ON-THE-JOB TRAINING

On the job training offers several options for training after the worker has accepted the position and is active in the assignment.

COACHING

This is a hands-on training experience whereby the trainer demonstrates the skill that is to be learned or improved. It requires that the trainer observe the trainee to offer specific instruction or correction along with feedback and analysis of the effort.

The coach might be a person you as trainer designate to do the training because they have an expertise you do not have. Computerization might be an example of such an expertise or some other very specific skill.

The four steps of learning McCurley and Lynch[22] detail are part of the coaching process:

1. **Experience:** learning from doing.

2. **Identify:** ability to describe the experience.

3. **Analyze:** ability to understand it as to how and why it happened the way it did.

4. **Generalize:** ability to draw from the experience some general rule or principle that can be applied to future situations. . .the transfer of learning.

Allow the trainee to set the pace in coaching. Do not overwhelm him or her with all that you know. Present several short demonstrations of various steps in any complex procedure, being careful to "read" the trainee to insure transfer of learning is taking place. Reinforce what the trainee does well and compliment it at the point they do it. Offer prompts when steps are omitted or incorrect. This brings them gently from their starting place to where you need them to be.

Insure that the four points of learning are experienced and integrated by the trainee, so that they learn from the experience of doing the task (not just observing it), can describe the experience (such as a sequential process), can analyze it in such a way as to understand how and why the task effort works, and can draw general principles from doing the task so that they can transfer this learning to future endeavors (such as good phone responses to callers, etc.).

COUNSELING

Counseling assists a person in solving a problem or doing a more effective job while having the trainee accept responsibility for the effort, rather than the trainer/counselor. It helps people being counseled to discover their own answers and solutions rather than having them provided.

Counseling empowers others and builds self-confidence and independence. It relies heavily on the counselor/trainer asking questions which challenge the trainee to find their own answers to problems. The questions, along with supportive information, allow the trainer to guide the learning while still encouraging the trainee to add their own creativity to conclusions. It is an enabling rather than a directive approach.

In the counseling process, the counselor/trainer can use the questioning-enabling approach to:

1. Identify what the problem is and is NOT.

2. Uncover the root or cause of the problem.

3. Create a list of response options.

4. Identify potential outcomes for each option (good and bad).

5. Choose the best option for action, with others ranked by effectiveness.

6. Design the steps necessary to achieve this option.

7. Examine the learning from this problem to avoid it in the future.

Counseling is really a form of consulting, that has as its goal, the increased effectiveness and confidence of the trainee and the ultimate success of the goal or effort. It must be done carefully so it does not intimidate the trainee while at the same time be strong enough to be trusted and direct appropriate action.

GENERAL TRAINING

General training, which can be held in-house in an organization or externally for different audiences, can be broken down into two sub-categories: Mixed audiences and Clustered audiences.

MIXED AUDIENCE TRAINING

After people have mastered the basic skills and actions required of their jobs, it is important to avoid the mistaken idea that training is completed. Because we live in the information age where each day brings incredible change, we must build continual training into our work. One way to do this is to offer people training that is advanced and often provided externally at a conference, area-wide workshop, college or technical setting.

This training, unlike the previous on-the-job varieties geared toward an individual or homogeneous group of job holders, is often aimed at a mixed group of trainees who are expected to translate the general information given to their own situations, asking themselves, "What does this have to do with me and my work?" It requires adult learning conversion skills to adapt data and be able to find use for it back on the job.

A workshop at a conference might, for example, be on "Trends for the Next Century" with John Naisbitt's *Megatrends 2000* used as one of the references. The audience might have 100 participants and the speaker may know little or nothing about the individual work of each of them but, if the information is solid, well presented and viable, it will have great value.

Each participant will be able to adapt the data and find connections to areas of work to be done. They may have an "ah-ha!" that clarifies a thorny problem that has been stumping them or an insight that changes how they are working.

Such training needs to offer:

1. Clearly defined data.

2. A challenge to find ways to use the data practically.

3. Opportunities to discuss or practice using the information by small group discussions with workshop peers.

4. Encouragement of questions and even challenges of the data.

5. An opportunity for participants to share creative applications with the rest of the group and be recognized for the creativity.

The challenge of the trainer in this type of session is enormous as the training must present a smorgasbord of information without overwhelming or intimidating the audience. It must allow for varied levels of competence and experience and field questions, challenges and even inappropriate responses at times. Each must be dealt with positively and with the goal of reinforcing the trainee while guiding, directing or redirecting the statements.

The trainer, to be effective, must:

1. Be flexible.

2. Know the subject backwards and forwards.

3. Be able to mix lecture, coaching, counseling and demonstration.

4. Be able to field any question or approach positively.

5. Attend to the different needs of the visual, auditory and experiential learners in the audience.

6. Glide between the directive (hard) approach and responsive (soft) approach to training.

All this and you'll still need to watch the clock for the break!

CLUSTERED AUDIENCE

Another variety of general training is when advanced skill building is offered to many people with the same job but in different settings. All of the managers of hospital volunteers, or all of the sales people selling the same type of product or all the student teachers in a school system are examples of such audiences.

For this type of training, the challenge of the trainer is to draw attendees in as partners who can offer peer-level examples and demonstrations of training points.

Encourage attendees to share success stories that illustrate key learnings or offer variations. Provide opportunities for learners to brainstorm together around learning points or simulated problems to encourage creativity. Avoid the appearance of singular, simplistic answers to problems and draw additional data and skills from attendees.

The key skill needed by trainers leading such events is gentle, persuasive control as participants are drawn into the training process. Problems that can arise and suggestions for handling include:

**PROBLEMS &
SOLUTIONS**

PROBLEM	POSSIBLE SOLUTION
1. Attendee rambles	1. Trainer stops them and prompts them to put ideas in order; uses flip chart to request numerically sequenced steps, forces attendee to organize thoughts.
2. Attendee skips to another point that should be discussed later in the training sequence.	2. Trainer interjects by using trainee's name and a statement such as "Jim, I'm going to ask you to hold that thought for now. . .we'll come to that point right after the break and I want everyone to really hear what you have to share." If you've given the audience learning points, you can point to where it will come and write "Jim" next to it to validate your intention to call on him then.
3. Attendee offers a bad example that would lead to disaster.	3. Trainer asks if anyone else has another example. If it's a good one, build on it, reinforcing its better demonstration of the point. If the first trainee persists, you might say "If that worked for you, I'm delighted, though others may wish to avoid that solution as inappropriate to their setting." Then explain why it might run into trouble elsewhere.

Keep in mind that there really is no "one way" to solve problems, so even the response you would avoid at all costs might actually be correct for someone, somewhere! (The *Never Say Never* philosophy of training!)

In all the format varieties for training, the critical factor for success is the well-equipped, informed and creative trainer who balances content and relationships, directive and support approaches and a deep respect for adult learners as partners in the training process.

Good training is never easy. . .but it is always worth the effort as you equip people with the skills, confidence and motivation to do assigned tasks and attain goals successfully.

It is the "stuff" from which miracles are made!

LEARNING METHODS

There are various learning methods which can be employed within the formats listed previously. Trainers often combine a "mix" of these methods to engage an audience and present information in a variety of ways to get their message across.

A solid understanding of adult learning is required of the trainer plus a familiarity of methods so that, as the trainer "reads" shifting audience needs, she/he can adapt and adjust by offering one or more of the following training options. I list them here with characteristics, suggested uses, positive and negative points, etc.:

LECTURE

1. Allows trainer to give a lot of information in a short time.
2. Demands great preparation and practice.
3. Can easily be "over-used" and thus abused or boring.
4. Does not allow for much (if any) feedback.
5. Gives trainer complete control over what is said (not what is thought, though).
6. Can be used well with very large groups.
7. Needs visual punctuation (flip chart, overhead, etc.).
8. Demands great vitality and stage presence of trainer.
9. Needs clear verbal examples to bring learning "home".
10. Appropriate humor helps ease the "sit-still-while-I-instill" effect.
11. Is enhanced by insuring that trainees can take notes easily (offer tables, etc.).

SKITS

1. Requires careful selection of skit actors. . .do not force people to act.
2. Can show contrasting actions (right vs. wrong, etc.) well.
3. Humorous actions can get lessons across.
4. Do not allow audience to ridicule or criticize actors. . .keep them focused on actions.
5. Be prepared to prompt actors if they falter.

DEMONSTRATION

1. Great learning if everyone can see/hear well, poor if not.

2. Allow participants to then practice skill, encourage creativity.

3. Be prepared to coach demonstrators if they falter.

4. Allow participants to share results of their attempts to duplicate demonstration.

VISUALIZING

1. Use only where audience has built solid trust in trainer.

2. Guide people gently, with simple instructions, step-by-step.

3. Do not force those who are resistant (the exercise has probably produced a painful memory or fear).

4. Allow people to proceed at their own pace.

5. Assign the task of a follow-up to visualization (i.e.: a letter written to themselves to be sent by the trainer 30 days after the seminar to remind them of their 30 day goal).

6. Insure confidentiality when appropriate.

PRACTICE

1. Provides opportunity to rehearse actions.

2. Can offer feedback from audience and/or trainers to sharpen a presentation, lecture, speech, etc.

3. Can build confidence of trainees by practicing skills such as a receptionist needs in answering a phone, directing people, etc.

4. Can provide ways to help people solve problems by having someone play role of person presenting a problem.

5. Can be used with small groups and assigned subject (i.e.: problem, challenge, work set-up, etc.).

6. Use carefully if participants are insecure. . .coach people gently toward appropriate responses and actions.

7. You can use video taping if deemed appropriate. This is especially helpful when training trainers.

PROBLEM SOLVING

1. Present problem in writing to small groups of participants and ask them to offer one or two solutions.

2. Have group share answers and discuss.

3. Have group prioritize best options for response and present to entire training audience.

4. You may find it valuable to group people by categories. (i.e.: Board members, upper administration, managers, line workers, volunteers, clients or consumers, etc.) to show different perspectives of same problem.

5. Emphasize the fact that all problems have more than one solution.

6. Offer written problem solving rules at start of exercise for guidance.

BRAINSTORMING

1. Lay out rules of Brainstorming:

   a. anything goes. . .creativity is encouraged.

   b. link ideas together for expansion. . .build on one another.

   c. play with ideas. . .go for quantity of thoughts with no evaluation.

   d. no one allowed to "shoot down" anyone's ideas.

   e. capture ideas so they don't get lost.

2. Use small groups (4-8) when possible.

3. Give any needed background information to get folks off to a solid start (too little data will set them up for failure/too much will direct them toward the "answer" they think the trainer wants).

4. High level managers can sometimes intimidate a group. . .people tend to defer to the boss . . . it is helpful to group people in peer settings.

5. Encourage fun . . . I often ask groups to write down ideas and tell them we'll count to see who has the greatest number in a given time. This encourages the quick responses I want. You can also offer a silly gift or reward for the most "off the wall" idea, etc.

DISCUSSIONS

Group discussions are the most commonly employed training method. To do them correctly the trainer must know how to stimulate, instruct and manage them well. (See Figure 4-1, p. 72, at end of chapter) Various groups take on varied characteristics.

1. **Whole group** discussions can work if the trainer can control the flow, draw people out, limit any rambling and keep the group on target. To do so the trainer needs:

   a. visuals available (flip chart, overhead, handout, etc.) to show progression of discussion point or pertinent information.

   b. to set time limits on discussion at start.

   c. to reinforce and highlight good points made from the audience.

   d. to sum up key points to bring leadership focus back to trainer.

2. **Small group** discussions are best when limited to 4-8 people:

a. give them clear instructions, reinforce by having them in writing on board, flip chart or overhead screen.

b. ask participants if they have any questions about the instructions.

c. have group appoint a facilitator, recorder and/or reporter.

d. allow people as much control as possible in forming their groups . . . you may suggest ways (all at one table, those in particular department, by years of experience, etc.) but allow them to decide on groups that "feel" right.

3. **Dyads or Triads:**

a. 2-3 people discussing ideas.

b. frequently does not require feedback from each set, but a general invitation from trainer for volunteers to share learnings.

c. useful when you are asking trainees to explore feelings or softer issues of relationships, visions, needs, etc.

4. **Experience sharing:**

a. having the audience share a particular problem and asking others to offer suggestions.

b. develop a list of options, since one can't work for everyone.

c. keep control of length and direction of responses. (See Figure 4-2, p. 73, at end of chapter)

d. if solutions are very complex, invite two participants to get together over break to match problem and solution, possibly reporting back to whole group later.

5. **Ice Breakers:** (See Figure 4-3, pp. 74-78, at end of chapter)

a. used to help people get to know one another.

b. must be used carefully — some people feel threatened or simply dislike them.

c. start simply — you'll be able to read the audience's acceptance/ rejection of this exercise.

ON-SITE VISITS

1. With smaller groups this can be invaluable as trainees observe work in progress.

2. Allow for questions to help trainees clarify what they are seeing.

3. You may want to assign tasks of observations to individuals (i.e.: "What technique was used by the worker to help the client?", etc.).

ROLE PLAYING

1. Must be carefully prepared in advance.

2. Do not simply grab people from an audience without their enthusiastic approval. Choose carefully.

3. Role playing in front of an entire audience needs to be rehearsed and coached before performance. Insure participants understand role and mind set.

4. Small group role playing is best when they employ three people . . . two roles and one observer . . . then have people switch places so that all parties take all three parts during exercise.

5. When people disagree on an issue, you might be able to have them reverse roles and debate from the opposite point of view. Be careful, however, I would not try this if there had not been a high degree of trust built in the session already!

CASE STUDIES

1. Present case study for groups or individuals to work on, then have them discuss response options.

2. Set time limits at start.

3. Offer any background information needed.

4. Write case studies from actual experiences you encounter so they do not sound contrived.

5. Encourage creativity . . . do not give the impression that there is one right answer to a study.

A good trainer understands and is able to use all of these learning methods, though usually prefer a few selected ones. Practice each method until you are comfortable with it and be able to extract it from your "bag of tricks" when called for.

And if all else fails . . . learn to tap dance!

THE LEARNING CLIMATE

The aura or climate that surrounds the training site, leader, and information is every bit as important as the training itself. This climate must be perceived as "user friendly" from the very first moment the trainees enter the room.

SETTING

To insure the proper training climate, the trainer needs to attend to the following:

1. When being asked or assigned to do a particular training, inquire about the **setting of the event.** If the answer is "Oh it's great!", don't leave it at that and assume that your definition of a great training room and the other person's are the same. Probe further.

   a. **Where is the room?** (hotel, office, etc.?) Beware "great" rooms at a motel that happen to be next to the pool — ten cavorting kids splashing with glee tend to be very distracting to audiences!

   b. **What size is it?** Avoid putting 10 trainees in a grand ballroom or a regular sized motel room from which the bed has been removed!

   c. **What set-up can be arranged?** (see Chpt. 6, p. 128 on set-up options) Avoid fixed-seat rooms. What non-trainers often call "great rooms" are the monstrous tiered "pits" with fixed tables and chairs on multiple layers. For trainers wanting people to mix and who need to interact with an audience, this can be a horror story.

   d. **What is the lighting?** Avoid windows behind the trainer that can't be draped, low "mood" lighting, spot lighting only and, generally, poor wattage that puts everyone to sleep.

   e. **Is there control over temperature?** Too hot or too cold is as deadly as poor lighting. Find out how it can be controlled.

2. Inquire as to where the training fits in the entire agenda and what **meal service** might be attached to the training itself.

   a. **Try to avoid heavy meals —** a person trying to learn marketing principles will have a more difficult time after a lunch of lasagna, meat balls, garlic bread, spaghetti, salad and hot fudge sundae (don't laugh, it happened in one of my sessions!) than following a light salad bar.

   b. **If breaks are to offer food,** arrange juice, coffee and fruit in the morning and soft drinks, coffee and something sweet in the afternoon.

TIMING

3. Ask about the timing of the session — seasonally, in the day and within the framework of the conference or work schedule.

   a. **Training held during hectic personal times** such as the holiday season, the week school opens, during traditional spring break times, etc., are very difficult both from the aspect of getting people to attend and that of keeping their attention when they have so many other agendas in their head.

b. **Avoid conflict with any and all religious holidays** (check both Christian and Jewish holy days), National holidays and cultural patterns (last and first week of school, summer vacation time, etc.).

c. **Look closely at your potential audience** — if they have patterns that might conflict, avoid them. (i.e.: a hospital scheduling a 100th anniversary celebration will not support a training event the week before; a business moving to new headquarters will not be ready for a conference during the move, etc.).

d. Trainings that will be full of heavy information (technical instruction, new procedures, radical change, etc.) are best at the beginning of the conference and in the morning when people are most fresh and alert. *Computer 843* doesn't go over very well at 4:30 on the 6th and last day of a conference! Try to **position what you are training** where it will be best received on the agenda.

e. **Find out what training has proceeded** your assigned topic and **what will follow it**. Work to build on what has gone before and help attendees transition to what will come later. Look for a natural, sequential flow. Recruitment fits naturally after goal setting and writing objectives; the reverse will be awkward and confusing — like teaching *Frosting 201* before *Cake 100*.

f. Keep in mind that a better word for "reality" is **"perception"** and if you are asking people to come to a training **whose timing offers deeply held perceptions**, you will have to work with them. For example, for a conference to be held in Minnesota, August was chosen as it fits into the perception of Minnesota offering cool weather, beautiful surroundings and relaxation to hot and harried workers around North America. The same conference set for January would offer an entirely different and difficult to market perception of ice, snow and grey, bitter cold. Conversely, Florida in January sounds great to a Chicago bound midwesterner such as myself — Florida in August does not.

In all of the climate factors listed above, you are dealing with how people "feel" either physically or emotionally. Physical comfort is a strange phenomenon-if everything is comfortable - room temperature, set up, furniture, lighting, breaks, etc. — participants will barely take note of them. However, if any or, heaven forbid, all of them are annoying or inappropriate, you can rest assured, you'll hear about them! They also will become an obstacle to learning and produce a mindset that is not conducive to accepting and interrelating information. Many an excellent trainer has been felled by a

95°, poorly lit room that is melting the gooey pecan rolls and candy bars while doing nothing to improve the cold coffee!

TRAINER'S INFLUENCE

A second aspect of the training climate is the aura that surrounds the trainer themself. In the first part of this book, I talked at length about the trainer's attitude, passion, preparation, etc.

Another factor that must be considered carefully is the trainer's demeanor before and during the training itself. A trainer who rushes in two minutes before the training is to start, brings handouts in a gym bag, forgets a magic marker and is frantically trying to reset the podium, flip chart and overhead projector, has probably already "lost" a good portion of the audience.

Optimists would say they would have no place to go but up in the workshop, but I think the opposite might be true. Trainers set the stage for their own acceptance or rejection which has a definite correlation to acceptance or rejection of the information that they impart.

SET THE STAGE

To insure your best chance at "setting the stage":

A. Arrive at least 30 minutes before the training is to begin

1. Rearrange the seating if it does not meet the needs of the training or groups-insure a clear view for everyone of the training "stage".

2. Arrange the training "stage" (that area of the room in which you as a trainer will conduct the session and in which your tools such as flip charts, lectern, projection screen, black board, etc., are located) so that it is in plain sight to everyone and is positioned for your ease of accessibility:

   a. Avoid having an overhead projector, for example, on the same level as the audience and down from the stage you'll use in speaking. This means you'll have to walk across the stage, down 2 or 3 steps and over to the projector each time you want to use or change an overhead - very distracting.

   b. Avoid having to walk between a projector and screen so that your shadow disrupts the image.

   c. Avoid having items you will use so far apart that your transition from one to the other is awkward and interrupts the training flow.

3. Check equipment carefully:

   a. Test microphones for feedback squawk, volume, sensitivity, "crackle" etc. If it's a podium mike, be prepared to be tied to it if the audience is very large. I prefer a clip-mike that I can wear on the lapel of a suit, etc. A hand-held mike is my second choice as I move around a lot in my presentations. For either of these two types, make sure that the microphone cord is long enough to accommodate your movement and be careful NOT to trip over it as you work! Use the same movement patterns while training that are carefully thought out so that you don't wrap the cord around the flip chart and then pull it over as you stretch out to reach the overhead! Have someone check for volume by going to the back of the room to see if you can be clearly heard. At the start of the training, you may want to test this out again with the audience and adjust the volume accordingly.

b. Make sure any site-wide PA systems are turned OFF to your training room. Having announcements about car lights on in the parking lot or calls for personnel to come to the office are a bit disconcerting in the middle of teaching Maslow's *Hierarchy of Needs.*

c. Test AV equipment carefully for position, ease of operation, mechanical demands and a back-up light bulb. I ask that a technician be present if a particularly demanding piece of equipment is being used (to me that means anything more complex that an orange on/off bar on the overhead or a Kodak Brownie camera!).

d. Locate the light switches and thermostat and create the physical climate you want. A rule of thumb for both: there is no such thing as too much lighting and cooler is better than warmer. If you're stuck with spot lights - place your podium and flip chart at the most intense sites - avoid the shadows at all costs.

BE FRIENDLY

B. Greet some of the first arrivals personally and in a friendly manner. Introduce yourself and find out a bit about them if possible. Set the stage by a conversational tone of voice. Be as relaxed as possible. Have LARGELY PRINTED name tags or table tents for everyone and wear one yourself that shows your first name (generally avoid other massive titles for yourself).

HANDOUTS

C. Insure that handouts are where they should be: at front of room near you if you like to hand them out selectively as you train; at people's seats or at back of room for folks to pick up as they arrive - it's your choice as to what fits best into your design.

CLOCK

D. Keep a clock in plain sight so you can follow the timeline. I always carry a travel alarm with me to set on the podium - it allows me to glance at it without interruption.

INTRODUCTIONS

E. Meet anyone who is to introduce you and make sure that they have their information correct and that they will mention whatever you feel your audience wants to know about you. I find that most people I train want to know my practical, in-the-trenches experience and probably could care less about academic credentials or honors.

DRESS

F. Dress appropriately. Know your groups well enough to know what this means — casual, more formal, business-like, etc. I tend to wear suits unless I know it is to be very casual such as at a retreat. Suits can be perceived as a great middle ground between slacks and sport shirts and 3-piece Cassini originals. I've seen a trainer "use" his suit to help an audience relax by starting the training with a statement of "I don't know about you, but by this time of a conference, I like to remove my tie and coat, roll up my sleeves and relax a little." He then proceeded to do just that as the audience followed suit and everyone took an audible deep breath.

In that one gesture, the trainer projected a "let's be friends – we're all in this together so let's relax" message that helped a positive – and receptive – mind set to be established.

After attending to the mindset, comfort, pace, set-up, and equipment aspects of a training, you can put your full focus on the learning itself. This attention to detail also allows the trainees to place their concentration on the training also, hopefully, allowing them to be ready for learning which must always be a major goal of any trainer.

A key point to keep in mind is that a trainer's goal cannot simply be limited to spouting information, you must also carefully orchestrate the climate to remove obstacles to learning and work toward the most conducive atmosphere possible.

WHEN THE CLIMATE IS ROTTEN!

A few words about the times every trainer encounters where the climate available is less then perfect:

It happens.
Adjust.
Keep you sense of humor.

I once had to train in a dirt floored barn in mid-Texas starting at 8:00 PM after participants drove in from churches as far away as 500 miles (yep, a ten-hour drive!). There were three 25-watt lights on cords hung from the rafters and the wooden seats, discards from a local mortuary, had had the rounded backs replaced by a straight horizontal board. My subject? *God's gift of volunteerism to the church!* Over one hundred weary Christians let me know ahead of time it better be good.

You should have seen me PRAY!

Arriving early, my co-trainers and I ran to town and bought clip-on flood lights to at least brighten the scene. We arranged for cheese, fruit, crackers, cookies and cold drinks (it was 95 degrees and humid). We arranged for tables to be brought in and set up for the next morning and when folks arrived at the conference site and signed in for their room, we met them there, got acquainted and told them we would not be working tonight, just setting the stage and getting acquainted. We urged them to dress casually, meet at the barn between 8:00 and 8:15, that we'd have snacks for them and break early for a good night's rest.

When assembled, we introduced our three-person training team, invited participants to have refreshments, introduce themselves to one another informally, etc. When everyone seemed relaxed, I asked them if we might not all be better able to really tackle the challenge of bringing volunteerism issues into the church if we rearranged our agenda to put our first workshop on in the morning. I also pointed out the ridiculous nature of our surroundings and asked for their help to make the barn the best it could be.

They resoundingly agreed and I invited them to share what they wanted and needed from our weekend together. Responses were recorded on a flip chart, the discussion was limited to about 25 minutes and we all went back to our refreshments or rooms feeling good and excited about the rest of our time together.

If you are a trainer for any length of time, you too will have your stories to relate of walking into what seems like an impossible set of circumstances for a learning environment.

The trick is to keep your wits about you, make it as positive as possible, acknowledging problems to the audience, draw participants into the challenge of making it as good as it can be and proceed.

After all, if Moses could carry his handouts on granite and speak to a multitude from a mountain side, what's a Texas barn or two among friends?

QUESTIONS TO ASK ABOUT A GROUP'S INTERPERSONAL PROCESS

1. **Do seriously intended contributions meet with no response?**

   Speakers need to know the effect of their remarks so that they can compare them with what was intended. When others do not respond, the speaker cannot know whether they (a) did not hear the comment, (b) did not understand it, (c) understood and agreed, (d) understood and disagreed, (e) understood but thought it irrelevant, or (f) felt uncomfortable because of the issue raised, etc.

2. **When a complicated, unclear, or controversial comment is made, does the group check to make sure it understands what the speaker means before agreeing or disagreeing?**

3. **Does each member state his personal reactions as his own rather than giving the impression that he is speaking for the group?**

4. **Are all contributions viewed as belonging to the group, to be used or not as the group decides?**

5. **When the group has trouble getting work done, does it try to find out why?**

   Symptoms of difficulty are excessive hair-splitting, points repeating over and over, suggestions not considered, private conservations in subgroups, two or three members dominating the discussion, members taking sides and refusing to compromise, ideas attacked before they are completely expressed, and apathetic participation. When such symptoms occur, the group should shift from working on the task to discussing the interactions and feelings of members about what is going on.

6. **Does the group blame its difficulties on *problem members*.**

   A group should look upon behavior that hinders its work as happening because the group wants it rather than blaming it on one or two *problem members*. The group should discuss what these symptoms indicate about the nature of the group problem — what is each of us not doing that perpetuates this condition?

7. **Does the group bring conflict into the open and deal with it?**

   Because of the difference between individuals, conflict is inevitable. The group can choose whether the conflict will be open (and subject to group control) or disguised (and out of control).

8. **Is conflict approached as a topic for joint inquiry into *What is best for us to do in this situation?* rather than as a competitive struggle to prove *Who is right and who is wrong?***

9. **Does the group make important decisions by open agreement or by default?**

   When the group views each decision as a provisional trail which can be carried out, evaluated and revised in the light of actual experiences, it is easier to make decisions than when each decision is required to be so perfect that it can stand forever without change.

   When the group agrees on a decision which it does not carry out, it should recognize that the real decision was not to act although the apparent decision was to act. The group should openly discuss why the apparent and real decisions were not the same.

10. **Does the group use different ways to make decisions depending upon the time available, the kind of issue, and the importance of the outcome?**

    A group may vote, delegate the decision to a certain person or subgroup, flip a coin, or discuss until they reach complete consensus. The crucial factor is that the group has complete consensus on the process used to make the decision in each case.

FIGURE 4-1

HOW TO HANDLE
AUDIENCE QUESTIONS: 9 TIPS

1. **Keep your question/answer brief.** Too much time spent addressing individual concerns lowers the *energy level* of the larger group. Stop the questions and close when you see the energy sag.

2. **Anticipate questions and try to prepare answers.** If it's a tough presentation, practice answering questions with a colleague in advance.

3. In answering the question, try to **reinforce key points** you've made in your talk. Avoid irrelevant tangents.

4. **Don't be afraid to rephrase** a question from a participant, or ask for more clarification.

5. **If you don't know the answer, say so;** then tell the questioner when you'll be able to get it to him/her.

6. **If you want time to put together an answer**, ask the questioner to repeat the question or even answer it him/herself.

7. **If you still can't answer the question**, ask it to other members of the audience. Say: "That's a good question. How do you feel about it?"

8. If a disruptive individual begins questioning you, he/she is probably looking for recognition. **Give it!** Say: "That's a good point." Then suggest you meet after the talk to discuss it further.

9. If you put aside a question and answer period, make sure you **leave time to summarize your main points** after the questions.

(Adapted from *Effective Business and Technical Presentations*, 2nd edition. George Morrisey, Addison-Wesley Publishing Company, Reading, MA, 1975.)

FIGURE 4-2

LET'S GET THAWED: ICE-BREAKERS AND WARM-UPS

The activities suggested below are generally helpful in at least three ways:

- as ice-breakers — "coming present," warming to the learning task at hand

- aids for the participants to get to know one another. People share more willingly and easily when they know the people with whom they are working.

- help in identifying group members as possible future resources.

And besides, these activities are fun. This list is just a beginning, and the length of your own list will grow with your experiences.

1. **Paired Introductions**   Each person meets and gets to know one other person and in turn introduces his partner to the entire group, including at least one positive personality trait which was noted about the partner.

2. **Dyad and Quartet**   Same as above, but instead of introducing his partner to the entire group, he introduces him to another dyad.

3. **One-Minute Autobiography**   Break into groups of ten or so. Each person is given one minute to tell about himself. Use a timekeeper, and don't let anyone go over one minute. Restrictions can be set as to what can be talked about (e.g.: nothing about job, family, home town, hobbies). These restrictions enable the participants to get right to attitudes and values.

4. **Structured Introductions**   In dyads, small groups, or in the large group, participants can write their own epitaphs, write a press release about themselves, write an ad about themselves.

5. **Life Map**   Each person draws on newsprint with crayons or magic markers a picture of his life, using stick figures and symbols.

6. **Name Circle**   Participants sit in a large circle. The leader begins by stating the name of the person seated to his right, followed by his own name. The person to his right repeats the leader's name, his own name, and adds the name of the person seated to his right. This process is repeated around the entire circle.

7. **Sandwich Boards**   Each person writes on a sheet of newsprint "Things I Know" (about the context and purposes of the workshop, areas of personal expertise, etc.). On a second sheet of newsprint, he writes "Things I Want to Know." The sheets are joined with tape, sandwich board style, and the participants mill around, non-verbally, identifying resources and getting to know one another.

8. **Sentence Completions**   A prepared list of sentence stems ("Anyone who smokes in front of his children". . .) is spun around the group or used in small groups.

9. **Pocket or Purse**   Each individual pulls out an item from her purse/his pocket and introduces her/himself in terms of this item, explaining why it is typical of her/him, etc.

10. **Thought Page**   A period of, say, five minutes is set aside for everyone to assign their thoughts, worries, whatever is on their minds to paper in the form of a list. Then all are asked to fold up the paper, put it away and let those worries or preoccupations be put aside for the time being, along with the piece of paper.

11. **The Zoo**   Each person decides what animal he would be if he had been born one. Then all like "animals" must find each other, congregate in groups and explain to each other why they "are" the animal they have chosen. Then, at the group leader's signal, all "animals" must make their animal's sound.

FIGURE 4-3 — p. 1

12. **Secret Share**   Each participant writes a "fun" secret about himself on a piece of paper. All papers are placed in a box or hat. Each person in turn draws a secret, reads it aloud, and says it was if it were his own secret, speaking in the first person. The group tries to guess whose secret it really is (a vote can be taken if necessary).

13. **What's My Bag**   (Advance notice to all participants is necessary for this one.) Everyone brings a bag (brown grocery sack is perfect) into which they have placed items that represent facets of their life, interests, job, hobbies, travels, etc. Each person takes turns presenting "their bag" to the group.

14. **True or False**   Everyone writes three statements about himself on an index card which he then pins to his chest. Only two of the statements can be true. Participants mill around, forming pairs, trying to decide which of their partner's statements are false. After each person guesses at which of his partner's statements is false, he puts a small "x" by that statement, the partners each move on to form new pairs and the process is repeated. At the end of this exercise, each person reveals to the group his own "x" tally, and identifies the two statements which are true.

15. **Picture Me**   Participants fold an 8-1/2" x 11 piece of plain paper in fourths. They then draw the following, one picture in each quadrant: something I do well; something I wish I did better; something I dream of (wish for); something I value. All pair off and explain what they have drawn to their partners. Each person then introduces his partner to the group in terms of the drawings.

16. **Name Game**   List letters of both your names vertically (or first name only if both your names are very long). Write an adjective describing yourself that begins with each letter of your name.

17. **Riddle de de**   Introduce yourself in terms of a riddle or limerick.

18. **Numbers Game**   The group leader asks all of those who are feeling like "10's" (fit as a fiddle and ready to go!") to raise their hands. The leader asks for the hands of 9's, 8's, 7's and on down to the point where everyone has identified their present "number" level of feeling. The leader huddles with the 10's, instructing them to each one go to a non-10 and through complements, smiles, and general positive attention, do what they can to help that person feel better. After a minute or two, the group leader asks the non-10 folks to indicate the number level they have risen to after the positive "stroking."

19. **Consensus-Based Group Objectives**   Each person privately lists five (the number is optional) personal objectives for the workshop. He shares them with a partner, and they arrive at five. The dyads go to quartets and then to octets. The octets report out their objectives (reached by consensus) and a total group set of objectives is formulated. This activity can aid in checking the contract and also help obviate the problem of hidden agendas.

VIPS/Little Rock, Arkansas

FIGURE 4-3 — p. 2

SENTENCE STEMS AS ICE-BREAKERS

I. Rationale

Used to gather information about people in a structured, non-threatening manner so that communication and trust can be established.

II. Explanation of Techniques

A. Seat participants in a circle in groups of 5-7.

B. Inform them that they have the right to "pass" if they cannot think of any answer when their turn comes.

C. Inform them that they have the right to say "no comment" if they choose not to answer.

D. Each person, in turn, answers or responds to a stem as he chooses to.

E. More than one person can have the same answer.

F. Rotate the person who answers the stem first each time.

G. Give a time limit for each stem (about 30 seconds or less per person in each group is average).

H. Process the event (see suggested process stems below).

III. Suggested Stems

The most beautiful (ugly) thing I've ever seen is . . .
What I like best (least) about me is . . .
My favorite movie (sport, hobby, place, holiday, etc.) . . .
I'm happiest when . . .
What I like best (least) about school (my family, my best friend) is . . .
Right now, the place I'd like to be is . . .
My greatest fear is . . .
My favorite hero is . . .
The ideal size for a family is . . .
One thing I do well is . . .
One way in which I need to improve is . . .
My favorite book . . .

Process Stems:
The person in the group I'm most like is . . .
The answer which surprised me most was . . .
A person in the group I'd like to get to know better is . . .
The image of myself I was trying to project during this activity was . . .

VIPS/Little Rock, Arkansas

FIGURE 4-3 — p. 3

WHO AM I LIKE?

Find someone in the group who:

1. Has the same number of brothers and sisters.

2. Was born under the same astrological sign.

3. Was born east of the Mississippi.

4. Can play a musical instrument.

5. Has the same favorite color.

6. Has the same favorite holiday.

7. Likes the mountains better than the beach.

8. Likes the city better than the country.

9. Has the same favorite hobby.

10. Has always lived in this state.

11. Drives the same make car as you do.

12. Had the same favorite subject in school.

13. Has gone to school out of state.

14. Has a secret desire to be a movie star.

15. Has the same favorite recording star.

VIPS/Little Rock, Arkansas

FIGURE 4-3 — p. 4

AROUND THE CLOCK

DIRECTIONS: Move about the room finding someone who answers these 12 items. When you find someone who fills the bill, put the name of that individual in the proper place. You can use a name only once!

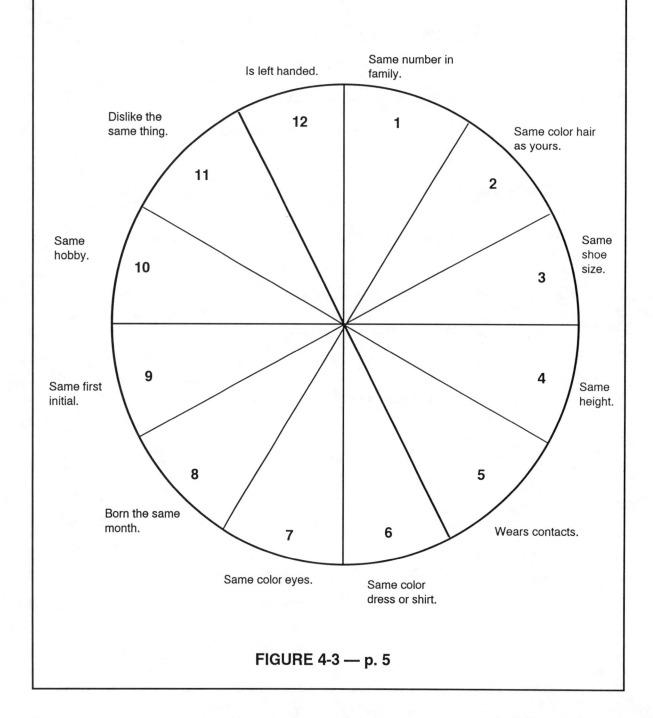

FIGURE 4-3 — p. 5

CHAPTER 5

PUTTING IT ALL TOGETHER: Planning, Designing and Executing The Workshop

For a trainer to accomplish the primary task of providing learning she/he needs to be three things rolled into one: the composer, the director and the performer! The tasks of the trainer can be broken down into three categories when we speak of workshops:

1. Planning.

2. Designing.

3. Executing.

PLANNING THE TRAINING

Training actually begins long before the trainer clips on a microphone and grabs a magic marker. It starts with the solid foundation of needs of an individual or group to learn, build skills or garner information.

NEEDS ASSESSMENTS

To help trainers (or event planners) start the process, a needs assessment must be activated. This might be as simple as a CEO or department head telling a trainer to plan for educating staff to a major change in the organization, new technology, new products or services, etc. etc. The defined need is in the demand of the "boss" and therefore must be heeded.

For such an example, the trainer begins with a mandate to offer identified training needs to people who must acquire skills or information. From this point it is critical to identify where potential trainees "are" in the learning cycle . . . are they completely ignorant of the subject? Is there some awareness and skill? Are some people proficient while others are totally non-skilled? What effect will the introduction of this new information have on trainees? Is the change going to be perceived as positive or negative?

INTERVIEW

To acquire this information you may choose the first option of needs assessment...the **interview**:

1. May be formal or informal, scheduled or non scheduled, spontaneous or casual,

2. An interview is really a conversation with a purpose or goal, therefore keep it on track and ask non-directive questions that allow the interviewee to give a response that is most revealing (interviews that are directive signal "right answers" to people; they often give you what the person thinks you want to hear) and candid responses.

3. Work to avoid being judgmental, defensive or leading. You want truthful answers that give you an honest look at issues.

If you are starting from a non-directed point (rather than a CEO telling you what to train) and want to find out what is needed, the following methods might be used in assessing needs:

SURVEYS

Surveys can be simple questionnaires or highly complex instruments. They can contain open-ended questions such as, "What would be most helpful to you as you do your work?" or offer multiple choices around the same question:

Check which would be most helpful in your work.

☐ Secretarial assistance

☐ More office equipment, (computer, fax, etc.)

☐ Financial assistance for further education

Surveys can even combine the two by offering a place for "other" in the multiple choice list. (See example, Figure 5-1, p. 100-102.)

SURVEY DESIGN

Surveys should be crafted carefully, reviewed by several people for additions, corrections or clarification and then tried out on a few people to see if they are effective. **Some tips on design:**

1. Keep your information goals clearly in mind . . . make sure all questions will serve this goal. Don't wander off on non-critical subjects.

2. Keep instructions for completion simple.

3. Keep wording simple.

4. List questions in logical sequence or clusters.

5. Be as non-directive as possible.

6. Be fair.

7. Keep the layout neat, clean and easy to read.

8. Clearly instruct those surveyed how and when they are to return the survey.

9. Provide a stamped return envelope if mailed out.

10. Guarantee autonomy but give OK to sign it if that is desired.

11. Coordinate with Computer Department if they are to be tallied by computer . . . have them help you design form and analysis report.

12. Be clear from the beginning on information you want (it's too late **after** the fact to extrapolate information not included in the survey design.).

OBSERVATIONS

You may simply want to quietly **watch activities** to analyze what is needed. Be careful to be fair in your assessment and very well informed . . . understand all ramifications of job demands before making a judgement about it. Involve people with varied perspectives as you observe . . . together all the perspectives should give you a balanced assessment. Never jump to conclusions, especially negative ones!

DATA REVIEW

You may want to simply **review** records, reports, history, past surveys, evaluation, board or management reports, meeting minutes, etc. . . . anything that can provide insightful data. Be careful about jumping to conclusions . . . sometimes simple additional facts can reshape your response to data.

GROUP DISCUSSIONS

You may uncover training needs simply by asking groups directly what would be helpful. At other times you may learn a great deal simply by listening to people express concerns as they gather in groups for other reasons (weekly management, evaluation or planning meetings, etc.).

SPOT CHECKS

Some trainers use the simple technique of talking to randomly selected staff, clients, workers, consumers or the general public to find out about perceptions, needs, wants, etc. You may conduct such an assessment to gather information you will use to augment training. For example, if you are planning a training on marketing a product, service, event or group, this method would help you uncover public perceptions on which to build further marketing efforts. You would then build this into your training.

PUBLIC OPINION

A very subtle form of needs assessment can be simply to gather insight and information from radio and TV talk shows, newspaper and magazine articles, expert testimony, newsletters, conversations, research, or reports that reflect public opinion. You may see trends emerging that can suggest the need for new training.

ANALYZE INFORMATION

After the needs assessments have been completed, the trainer must ANALYZE and evaluate the information. The raw data should be examined from the aspects of:

1. How the information relates to the goal of the assessment.

2. What the data means to the organization or program.

3. Where training needs are apparent.

4. Where trainees are presently and where they need to be.

5. What related trainings have touched the same subject.

KNOW YOUR AUDIENCE

After the need for training has been determined and sketched out, it is critical to KNOW YOUR AUDIENCE.

1. Who needs the training?

2. Who will attend?

3. What are their jobs, positions, roles?

4. What training have they had in the last year or so?

5. Have they ever had training on this same subject?

6. Will they come to the training voluntarily or as mandated?

7. What is their experience or competency level?

8. What is the attitudinal climate of the audience?

9. What relationships do the attendees have with one another?

HOW WERE NEEDS DETERMINED?

If you are being hired by a workshop planner or manager, carefully investigate **how this person determined needs, chose topics and contacted you** among other trainer. I'm cautious about someone hiring me without input on needs from people who will be part of the audience . . . occasionally the person has a desire to force an opinion or position on trainees that reflects a personal rather than an organizational stance. They hire a <u>trainer</u> to do their talking for them! Such cases rarely reflect what the audience or organization perceives as a need at all. Remember of course that your client is the organization that hired you - you are not there to reflect one person's crusade.

Always avoid being set up to play "puppet" for a hiring person. You'll recognize this tactic when they begin to try to script you, telling you what to say or not say. That's a "trap" that sets you up for failure almost every time. Just say, "Thanks, but no thanks" when such an invitation comes your way!

GET FACTS

Ask the contact person or manager requesting the training the following questions beyond those about the audience:

1. What is the goal for the training. . .the desired outcome? How does this relate to the goals of the organization?

2. What is the time frame available?

3. What topics are to be included? (Do not accept answers such as "trends" or "marketing." Ask them to explain what they mean by these words. "Trends" to one person can mean something very different to another.)

4. Fees and budgets, if applicable to your situation.

5. Location of training and expected size of audience.

6. Materials required when (manuals, handouts, etc.)?

7. Who decided on the need for this training?

8. Will your training be part of a larger conference? If so, what else is being offered? When? Will there be workshops opposite and in competition to yours?

9. Who will be your contact as you design and implement the training? Who will handle logistics?

10. What information/materials are required of you prior to the workshop (bio, photo, outline, goal statement, formal title of workshop, etc.)?

11. What other, if any, demands will be placed on your time around the workshop (reception, banquets, board meeting, photos, etc.)?

SITE

If you are personally in charge of the site for training, read carefully through the section in this book on climate . . . the setting of the training event is as critical as the content and needs to enhance rather than detract from the learning.

If you are offering an intense workshop, you may wish to choose a SITE that is removed from the hustle and bustle of a city . . . a place where participants can fully concentrate on the subject and not be tempted to run over to the office during breaks. You may even wish to choose a site that demands that people stay overnight in the facility if the workshop is to be a multiple day event.

In choosing your site, consider what climate you wish to build for the group. Keep in mind that the fewer the distractions and interruptions, the better the learning will be for participants.

Planning of a workshop is critical to its success. The better the planning, the better the final learning product. Time spent in this aspect is an investment in success.

DESIGNING THE TRAINING

The design of the training follows the planning, which continues to weave through the creative process. With the analysis of the needs in mind, the trainer begins to put form to the design.

Whether or not I am developing a workshop (which might mix several subjects) or a content component on one subject, I include the following:

1. Goal of training — learning objectives.

2. Logistical information — time frames with breaks noted; room set up; audience size, group buzz words if designing a client workshop, etc.

3. Key learning to present — listed in sequential order.

4. Key notes — basic information for each key learning — critical issues to impart.

5. Training options — lecture, exercises, overheads, flip charts, activities, etc.

6. Experiential examples — war stories, quotes, etc.

7. Bibliographical and resource materials — handouts.

From this overview of the training, I physically create my classroom notes. Let me share a sample overview here with my comments on each component listed to the right:

INFORMATION	COMMENTS
Title: *Marketing Magic For Nonprofits In The 90's*	Title is critical to marketing and audience expectations!
GENERAL INFO: Client: Girl Scouts of Washington, xx Date: Sept. 15, 19xx Location: Holiday Inn, Washington Room: Banquet Hall - round tables w/6 Audience: 30 GS leaders (troop coord) Times: 9am-3pm. 1 break & lunch Terms: Troop Leaders, Area Reps, Troop Coordinators	Try to get lunch served away from meeting room; folks need change; too confusing. Use titles for their group.
GOAL: To acquaint people w/marketing principles to use in volunteer recruitment and fund-raising . . . must raise $50,000 by March 15th to fund camperships and troop activities. Dues do not cover present costs.	Clear cut and achievable in time frame with this size audience.

INFORMATION	COMMENTS

KEY LEARNINGS:
  A. Marketing is caring trade of value
     for value
     1. Publics. . .trends
     2. Markets. . .targeting
     3. Trade of values. . .exchange
       relationship
  B. Fund-raising is Friend-raising
     1. Motivation. . .Vroom,
       McClelland, Maslow
     2. Art of asking. . .strategizing, 4 steps
       a. what have to trade?
       b. what need?
       c. who has it?
       d. how get it?
  C. Practical application . . . plans of action
	Here are the major points I want to get across if all else fails
	
	Transfer of learning

After this overview is jotted down, I create my classroom notes as follows (please note my comments to you, the reader, in right hand column):

KEYNOTES (Sample)

CLIENT: Girl Scouts
TIME: 9-12; 1-3pm
INFO: titles: troop leader; area rep. "council coord"

LOCATION: Washington, IL
COORDINATOR: Annette Esser
TITLE: "Marketing Magic"

SYMBOLS KEY:

🖳 = Overhead		Q = Quote	
🖳 = Flip Chart		XXXX = War Story	
⌣ = Group Exercise			
☺ = Individual Exercise			

TIME	VISUALS	CONTENT	EXERCISES	COMMENTS TO READER
9:10 a.m.	🖳 Q "If you can dream it, you can do it."	OPENING: Herman Cartoon • tough job to manage today • let's learn practical skills today • what are biggest challenges? • process and categorize – ✓ off those we'll do today • tell them how to use handouts	Whole Group 🖳	When first training, your notes may be long – later key words will remind you of content. You'll flush out info. (my overheads and handouts also act as my prompts.)
9:30 a.m.	🖳 "caring trade" 🖳 Gallup Info	Marketing is not a four letter word – caring trade of value for value TRENDS: • extinct volunteer "Polly DoGooder" • why people volunteer? • facts – Gallup Poll • how marketing works to recruit	Polly 🖳 Whole Group 🖳 SD Story	• I use the cartoon on flip chart to warm audience and get a lot of statistics over gently. (Also sets tone of fun) • Drives home hard concepts of Marketing Avoids resistance and helps transfer of concepts. War Story of example
10 a.m.	🖳 Public's Chart	Publics – identifyable segments of society	⌣ Publics List (15 min)	• I show example – groups list publics in their area. • Tell them we'll see who lists most – spurs them on. (Brainstorm Technique)
10:20 to 10:40 a.m.		BREAK		
		How to create "Public File" – why?	draw for them 🖳	Bridge back after break to bring folks to where we stopped. Show how/why of doing a Publics file.
	Markets 🖳 🖳 Exchanges	Markets – targeted publics to have what you need Exchange Relationships – value trades	"What offer volunteers?" (8 min) ☺	Here's where I ask them to create personalized ideas for recruitment/marketing.
	🖳 McClelland 🖳 Maslow 🖳 Vroom 🖳	FRIEND RAISING/MOTIVATION 1. McClelland – affiliation, power, achievement 2. Maslow *Hierachy of Needs* 3. Varoom's *Theory of Expectancy*	GS Story Classify jobs ⌣ List expec-tations ☺ share with group	War Story Helps them translate theory to real life work Do on own – then share
Noon		Instructions for lunch – what we'll do in p.m.		Helps bridge to afternoon

TIME	VISUALS	CONTENT	EXERCISES	COMMENTS TO READER

1 p.m.	Art of Asking
	4 steps
	Have?
	Need?
	Who has?
	Grp. Feed-Back
		Art of Asking – Characteristics
		• 4 step process:
		1. what do you have?
		2. what do you need?
		3. who has it?
		4. how do you get it?
		   a. strategy options
		   b. door openers?
		   c. timing?
			CF story
			what need?
			who has?
			"need 5000 2-color brochures"
				After bridging them back to the topic I use a story to get their attention.
				
				Then I break them into groups to move them around – highly inter-active to stimulate them after lunch.
				
				draw group into design of action plan around hypothetical need.

2 p.m.	Action Plans	Action Plans – describe/show example Trainees Practice – report back to group.	or 20 min	Transfer of learning to practical application.
2:30 p.m.		Feedback – Wrap-up: Polly's dead 4 Steps Mktg. definition Fund-raising is FRIEND-raising		Wrap up all key points here Group questions answered
3 p.m.	Q "If you can dream it you can do it."	You CAN do it! Motivation – Send off – reference to handouts and bibliography for further reading		Tied training together by using opening quote again here.
3:15 p.m.		Evaluations (done by host)	EVAL	Stay at back of room if people want to chat.

This KEY NOTES format is what I have in front of me while training. It supplements thoughts on overheads or in handouts which I also use as notes. The notes are developed from the training overview shared previously — the overview is my content design.

The design of the workshop or subject component needs to be carefully done. It must be crafted with flexibility balanced against key learnings that must be imparted even if your time is cut in half!

With practice, trainers are able to blend the learning points in easily while keeping the participants involved, alert and eager to learn.

EXECUTION OF TRAINING

I'm not sure I'm wild about the word "execution" when talking about the management of the training itself, but let's just agree we understand that it has nothing to do with arranging for the demise of either the participants or the trainer!

In the execution of the training you are adding life to it, where as in designing it you were creating the form. To bring this life about, you must juggle many different skills, needs and experiences to realize real learning.

I have listed many workshop management tips in the "Comments" column of the Marketing Workshop example shared in the previous section. Beyond them, however, are some more general guidelines for workshop management.

ELEMENTS OF TRAINING

In Arlene Shindler and Dale Chastain's excellent booklet, *Primer for Trainers*[23], the authors list six elements of training that must be present for learning to occur. Though discussed in greater detail elsewhere, it may be helpful to list them again here:

1. The learner must be involved.

2. There needs to be a demonstration of the skill.

3. There should be an opportunity for learning.

4. It needs to be presented in logical sequence.

5. It must be presented in various ways.

6. Skills already learned can be adapted.

These components: "involvement, demonstration, practice, sequence, repetition and adaptation . . . are elements of successful teaching, whether occurring in the workshop or classroom," Schindler and Chastain state.[24]

WORKSHOPS VERSUS CLASSROOM

Workshops vary from the regular classroom, however, by the following differences:

1. Little or no ability to assess the skill or competence levels of participants.

2. Little ability to assess effect of learning after the event . . . did the information build skills? Make a difference? etc.

3. There may be great variances in characteristics and competency of attendees.

4. Participants may have very different needs for learning.

5. Participants may come with different assumptions about what they will be learning.

6. Participants may be quick to judge the training for relevance and/or the trainer for credibility.

7. Some participants may know more than the trainer.

8. Participants may not all want to be there.

EXPECTATIONS

The trainer must make clear and keep in mind why the participants have been called together. It is critical for the trainer to uncover the audiences' expectations and assumptions about what they will learn. If you are training for a client that has marketed the event, be sure to see the marketing pieces to assess what has been promised.

If you find that the workshop has been promoted inappropriately and the attendees promised something you did not plan on providing, you have two choices:

1. Work to realign the audience.
2. Work to realign your presentation.

There is no hard and fast rule from which to choose, though the energy for the first is often higher than that of the second.

If you choose to readjust the audience, time is a critical factor. If a first marketing piece is a teaser, you can renegotiate with the planner to more clearly and accurately market it in subsequent efforts.

If it has been announced in the only marketing piece planned, and the workshop is only a week away and the information is so"wrong" (you don't train the subject advertised or it promotes an incorrect concept such as "Volunteers Are More Trouble Than They Are Worth!" or "It's Easy to Sell Our Product. . .Only the Lazy and Stupid Fail!," etc.) that you cannot be associated with it, your only options are to refuse to appear or do so but tell the audience at the start that there has been a shift in subject.

Try to avoid the non-appearance, everyone loses when that occurs. Be prepared to have a lot of your audience walk out when you tell them of a subject change. Be careful not to blame anyone for the problem, but be truthful about there having been a mix up in communication on the topic for the workshop.

If you think it is wiser, and possible, to change to the topic advertized, do so in such a way that the audience never knows the difference. Do, however, discuss the mixup with the conference planner to insure it does not happen again. I've had several occasions where I showed up at a conference only to find some committee changed my topic or title and forgot to notify or consult with me on the change. In each case I've been able to pull a rabbit out of the hat and adjust, but I've never felt that the training was as good as it could have been had I had more than five minutes notice of the topic! (I would never train, however, in a topic with which I was not familiar.)

WORKSHOP FLOW

The task of the trainer at the workshop itself is to **manage the flow of information** so that it goes logically from point to point. When natural breaks happen, such as lunch, forming into small groups, questions, etc. help the audiences' transition over the break, bringing them back to the information flow, by reminding them of where they were prior to the interruption.

BRIDGING

When there is a shift from point to point or topic to topic, the trainer needs to BRIDGE the two separate entities by pointing out the relationship between the subjects. This is enhanced if your natural style is to train sequentially in logical fashion.

You will also use BRIDGES when, during the workshop flow, you want to tie one idea to another. You might do so by reminding participants on day three of an event or statement from day one, thus tying the ideas together.

When training on a faculty for a multiple day and subject seminar, I try to sit in on the workshops offered by others to take notes on what I might interweave into my presentation when it becomes my turn to present.

ACCORDIONS

Schindler and Chastain talk in their booklet about ACCORDIONS, which they define as "activities that can be stretched, squeezed or eliminated depending on time available and the experience of participants."[25]

To facilitate such ACCORDIONS, I have developed a pattern of creating my training notes using several columns that denote time frames, key learnings, resources, AV and aide options, exercises and handouts (see example, page 87-88). I am constantly deciding what to use, when to use it and how long to take, based on time, audience needs and expertise.

To be frank, I've never come out exactly to the minute for what I've planned to teach because trainees needs cause constant adjustments, but I've also not left out key learnings which are the reason we are gathered together, and am rarely beyond my time constraints by more than 3-5 minutes, if at all.

This comes as the result of knowing what can and cannot be squeezed or eliminated in training. The one rule I impose on myself is to never skip a key learning point and be flexible with everything else!

CONCLUSIONS

The last bridge that is built by the trainer is one that spans the entire learning, tieing it all together to bring attendees back to the big picture and away from the individual parts that make up the whole. You can see this in my marketing example (page 87-88) in the previous section as I help the audience return to why we gathered, what we learned, key points and issues, and a final motivational send off to assure them they can do it. I closed with the same quote, you will note, with which I opened, to tie it all together in the last sentence.

The same thing can be accomplished by a running theme throughout a presentation — a visual, an analogy, a single illustration or case study or a commonly understood parallel — anything to bond it together as a whole and bring it to a conclusion.

PRESENTING INFORMATION

We've talked elsewhere about options in training and I'm hopeful that you have developed a sizeable "bag of tricks" of techniques to offer audiences.

If you've ever had to sit through a speaker who uses only lecture, only role play or any other singular approach, you know how deadly this can be for any length of time.

My point here is to convince you to plan to vary the activities within the training time and to have in the back of your mind many additional methods you can use should your planned activities not meet audience needs.

GIVING INSTRUCTIONS

When offering information through participatory methods such as dyads, triads, group or individual exercises, be sure that you give CLEAR IN-STRUCTIONS.

To back up your verbal directions, also offer them in writing — on handouts, at the top of tests, surveys or other written materials — anything they are to fill out or use as the base of discussion. When written materials are not involved, place instructions on a flip chart, blackboard or overhead transparency so individuals and groups can refer to them as they work through their assignment.

In giving instructions, provide:

1. Goal of exercise and relevance to workshop content.

2. Step by step instructions in sequential order.

3. Method to be used . . . small group, with partners, silently, etc. and the logistics of the exercise . . . i.e.: "You might just want to work with people at your table."

4. How it will be shared (or that it won't be shared, but kept private).

5. If group will need a leader, recorder, reporter, etc.

6. Time length given for activity.

7. What will be accomplished when the task is completed.

8. Opportunity for participants to ask for any clarification they might need.

As time to end the exercise draws near, give them a gentle reminder: i.e. "you have just one more minute on this."

If the group divided into dyads (two people) and the task requires each to talk one-half of the allotted time, tell them when the halfway point is about to come so they can switch from one person to the other.

A quick word about the instruction that tells the audience how it will be shared: If you are asking the audience to complete an exercise that required them to work on a deeply personal or confidential area, assure them at the start that you will NOT be asking them to share their thoughts with anyone.

As I train in life-balance and wellness issues and help audiences sort through personal stress, burnout, over-functioning, anger, etc. I frequently ask them to evaluate themselves around these sensitive issues. I have them do some of this work in writing but assure them several times during the instructions that they will not have to share it with anyone in the workshop . . . this helps them be more candid in their self-appraisal.

On occasion, I will ask them to think of people, places, things, etc. that are stressful or helpful, depending on the exercise. At the time of instruction I will tell them that I will ask for volunteers to share **categories** regarding their individual answers but not **names**. I also assure them no one will be forced to speak.

Understand that when I present such an instruction, I am prepared if NO ONE wants to share their list. When this happens, I switch quickly to offering categories of helpers or stressors that the group can discuss theoretically.

PROCESSING

As small groups are working on a task, I walk among them, making myself available to reinforce or clarify instructions. I am also doing a bit of eavesdropping so that when I am orchestrating group responses, I have an idea of what might be coming from various corners. This also helps me when I am assisting the audience in PROCESSING information . . . a critical role for any trainer.

As PROCESSOR, you will select, clarify and direct participants contributions, bringing what is shared into the workshop context and relevance. As you walk among groups or present yourself during the processing segment of the learning, be careful to remain nonjudgemental. It is helpful to understand group processing skills and interpersonal relations as noted in Figure 4-1, p. 72, of Chapter 4 to aide you as you work with groups. Try to refrain from intervention unless you hear confusion as to task, instructions, etc. or if they have gotten off on a wrong track due to misinformation or incorrect assumptions.

TRAINER'S ROLES

As you manage the flow of the workshop, you will wear several different hats as you act in different roles demanded by the content and audience.

At times you will be the EXPERT, offering data and information for participants. At other times you will be the FACILITATOR who orchestrates and processes information exchanges between everyone present, including yourself. Paraphrasing, synthesizing, clarifying, adding missing pieces of information, redirecting and selecting the best and most appropriate responses from the many offered, is part of this FACILITATOR/PROCESSOR role.

The third role you may adopt and one I use most frequently along with that of Facilitator, is that of INQUIRER, who ask questions, seeks information and asks people to share ideas, etc.

I believe that all three roles can be combined expertly and remain true to adult learning principles when the Facilitator and Inquirer are dominant and the Expert is played out with a **lack** of arrogance.

Certainly there are times when you will need to offer information such as statistical data, regulations, etc. that force you into an Expert role, but even these can be done in a manner that rejects an authoritarian aire. For years I have been giving audiences the latest statistical data on modern volunteerism that are specific facts from demographic research, but I have been doing so by using a cartoon of a stereotypical female volunteer I call Polly Do-Gooder.

Audiences accept Polly in great good humor and are mainly unaware that I'm giving them expert information in a friendly, versus authoritarian, manner. Because I begin many trainings with Polly, it also sets the stage for my use of humor and my preference for a relaxed climate during the training.

Throughout the management of any workshop or training event, you will need to remain flexible and responsive to the changing needs of your audience. You will need to set the climate, move among your various roles comfortably, draw the audience in appropriately, ease transitions and breaks and keep the flow of information running smoothly and logically from point to point to conclusion.

As mentioned elsewhere, this will require you to think in about ten different directions simultaneously and be ready at a moment's notice to shift gears.

The goal is the real learning of the participants and their confidence in the workshop leader. Work to downplay focus on yourself as you increase the focus on the information, so that participants go away confident that what they have learned is valid, practical and effective.

The trainers role, like the beautifully crafted frames surrounding museum masterpieces, is one of definition and direction that has observers focus on the beauty and quality of the information within the framework of the training. It is inappropriate and even detrimental for the trainer to want the focus to be on them and their performance. It is appropriate for the trainer to be a gentle but unobtrusive guide in the art of learning.

EVALUATIONS

Years ago, when I began to train within an organization, I developed a habit that would haunt me for decades. At the end of each training (small groups of up to 25 people, having to learn how to lead walkathons . . . a new concept my organization was bringing to America) I would ask participants to evaluate my training. Was everything clear? Did they understand everything they were to do? Could I have shared anything more effectively? What did I not do well in the training? etc.

Of course, with those questions so inappropriately focused on **me**, and including impossible standards of perfection ("everything," "anything") , someone always found something not to their liking or needs. What should I have expected since I was directing respondents to give only **negative** feedback!

After reading these evaluations, I agonized over every word. Never mind that 24 people had ranked the training an overall 10 out of 10, or that 99% of the comments were great. I lost sleep over the 1% and flogged myself for "failing."

After becoming an independent trainer, I continued this suicide pattern so that if one person out of 100 chided me for some "failing" I focused on the one contritely and ignored the satisfaction of the 99!

The grey hair you see adorning my head was probably caused in great part by this foolishness, but now I use it as a symbol to remind myself that with maturity comes wisdom (hopefully . . . sometimes . . . maybe).

The wisdom I've earned grey hairs for is simply this:

KEEP EVALUATIONS IN PROPER PERSPECTIVE!

REDEFINE EVALUATION

First of all, reshape your definition of "evaluation" by substituting the word "suggestion" for it. Then realize that those "suggestions" are opinions that you can act on, accept, file in the "interesting file" or throw away with the trash.

One person told me in all earnestness once that I should eliminate all humor, casual conversational tones and war stories in my training, so that I would seem valid to audiences. She said it with a straight face that I suspect always had been "straight" and never wrinkled by smile lines. I nodded positively and told her I would certainly consider this . . . as she walked away, she turned to add, "Good, I'm glad I've helped, and if you really want to be known as an authority, get a Doctor's degree in something!"

Great idea . . . think I'll write my thesis on "Confessions from Over Functioning Seriousers" or "Theoretical Data Analysis Regarding the Glum-Glums of our Planet." I'll make it into a book and have Irma Bombeck write the Forword. Hmmmm... .

Keep in mind that evaluative comments reflect opinions of an individual who may have been forced to come to the training, had the car break down six blocks from the building and had to walk the rest of the way in a pouring rain, ruining an expensive pair of shoes! Believe me, nothing short of a miracle would put that person in a positive frame of mind.

I'm reminded of a training I did on a rainy day in a very economically depressed area of another state that went very well except for three folks sharing one table. All day they groused about everything . . . the chairs, the room, the handouts, the soft drinks, etc., etc.

I wondered what they would say on their evaluation and was glad they'd left the training room when I glanced at their comments which were all good when discussing the content, but ended with:

"I'd expect more common sense from a national trainer than to have held this training during a rain storm."

I came down with a case of the giggles on that one and understood the rain storm gave them a way to vent their frustration at the economic climate in which they were barely surviving. Bless their hearts . . . I hope it helped them release some of their anger and actually pray it never occurred to them that the training had been on the calendar for nine months . . . rain storm or not!

DESIGN   When designing evaluations for training or assisting conference planners to do the same, keep the following in mind:

1. Aim questions at training content and presentation, not trainer personality.

2 Craft fair, not loaded, questions.

3. Word instructions and questions simply and clearly.

4. Keep it short. . . use check-off format as much as possible.

5. Offer space for comments.

6. Do not demand people sign their name (but permit it if they choose).

Figure 5-2, p. 103, is one of the forms offered for seminar evaluation in the book *Evaluating Volunteers, Programs and Events*[26]. It also offers a sample evaluation form for large conferences that are a variation and expansion of these same principles. Additional samples of evaluation forms are offered here in Figures 5-3, 5-4, and 5-5, pp. 104-106.

Allow the participants enough time to complete the evaluation at the end of the workshop, or at the end of each of its segments if that is your or the coordinator's choice.

DISSEMINATION   At this point I must admit to a quirk I have about evaluations: I never read them on the day I've trained. It's not that I'm afraid to, it's just that I'm usually exhausted at that point and personal criticisms that I can put in perspective at a later time, can make my blood pressure rise. I wait a day or two until I'm rested, then look them over. Frankly, I discount two categories: those that say I walk on water and those that say I'm an agent of the devil because I dye my hair (I don't, but one participant thought so and assigned me to the guy with the red cape once!). Both are too extreme and probably reflect some state of mind of the evaluator, not the real content of the training.

I have a dear friend, who is an outstanding trainer, that says she never even looks at evaluations unless she's trying out new material. She claims SHE knows if the learning objectives were accomplished better than anyone in the room, so she thanks the event coordinator profusely then deposits them in the next recyclable paper bin she sees!

How you choose to use evaluations is up to you. I prefer to see them as opinions I can use or lay aside as I plan future trainings. When developing a new training subject, I work hard to examine all the comments carefully and work to refine it to be the best it can be.

**STAYING IN
FOCUS**

And that brings me to my final point on evaluations:

✦ Do the BEST you can with the circumstances you're given . . .

✦ ACCEPT COMMENTS AS OPINIONS, not absolutes . . .

✦ FEEL GOOD ABOUT YOUR BEST EFFORTS, then go home and . . .

✦ TREAT YOURSELF TO THE BIGGEST HOT FUDGE SUNDAE KNOWN TO HUMANITY!!!

Evaluation is a critical part of helping us make our training be the best it can be. It is a positive tool if used positively.

When it becomes a negative tool you use to flog yourself, you've missed the point and it will cause an unnecessary energy drain.

Training is the only job in town where you are "graded" every time you work. If CEOs, teachers, doctors, secretaries, clerks and generals had to face the same standard, they would probably shrivel up and die on the spot, or at least shrink a lot!

Be kind to yourself . . . use evaluation as a positive tool for growth and learning. Make it your friend, not your adversary!

PROBLEM TRAINEES

Yes, you will run into one or two of these on occasion. When it happens, put them in their proper perspective against the backdrop of the 99.9% of attendees who have benefited from your training and added rich and positive dimension to the workshops.

In other sections I have offered specific options in dealing with people who present challenges to you as a trainer. I've also collected several examples from articles and writings from different sources that offer great tips, diagnostic information and productive responses for you to consider. See Figures 5-6 through 5-9, pp. 107-115, at the end of this chapter.

Keep in mind that a big part of your job as a trainer is to manage the flow of the workshop. This includes managing the people who make up the audience, and when problems arise in dealing with them, avoid the temptation to "fix" them if it is going to be at the expense of the rest of the audience.

**AVOID POWER
STRUGGLES**

I've watched inexperienced trainers get hooked into a power struggle with a participant where they wasted valuable workshop time playing word games with them. Audiences can be your best ally in restraining excessive demands or attention getting from a participant . . . asking how many of the other trainees wish to have the question addressed that is raised by one person is a trick of the trade most trainers use. In 99% of the time, the answer from the audience to such a question is "no" we're not interested, which gives you the opportunity to move on.

INTERRUPTERS

If a person persists in disrupting a workshop, I find addressing them directly and telling them we can talk privately at the break or, in extreme cases, delivering this message along with walking over to them and touching their shoulder, gets the message across. Only once did I have to go to a really strong response of asking the event coordinator to remove this person from the audience after continual, and totally inappropriate interruptions of myself and everyone else who spoke from the audience.

In that case it was clear we were dealing with a disturbed individual, and there were audible sighs of relief when I took the action I did. I tried to take that action as gently as possible, then, when the person was removed, I suggested everyone stand and take a two minute stretch break before we returned to our learning. After this break I went back and re-sketched what we had been learning to that point, what the progression of key concepts was and where we were in the process. This gave both the audience and myself time to catch our breath, refocus on our learning objectives and move on from a painful interruption.

Audiences do challenge our creativity and people-management skills as we train, but this is part of the role we accept when we become trainers . . . no one ever promised us that training would be easy!

Training Needs Assessment
State Family Programs
July 1990

The following information is being collected for use in designing the content of a training session on volunteer management for State Family Programs personnel. Your responses will be utilized to make the training as specific and as useful to your concerns as possible. Please answer the questions as completely as you can and feel free to add any additional comments or suggestions that you think would be helpful. For questions that ask for numerical answers, feel free to use an approximate number as a response.

1. Approximately how many volunteers are currently involved in your Family Program? Approximately how many Family Support groups are operating in your state?

2. What do you see as the major benefits to utilizing volunteers in your program?

   A.

   B.

   C.

3. What do you see as the major problems or barriers to utilizing volunteers more effectively?

   A.

   B.

   C.

4. How would you describe the attitudes and involvement of other National Guard staff on working with volunteers?

5. What are the three most interesting or useful types of jobs that volunteers have performed in your Family Program during the past year?

   A.

   B.

   C.

FIGURE 5-1 — p. 1

6. What volunteer recruitment techniques have proven most effective for you?

    A.

    B.

    C.

7. Are there any particular groups or organizations that have proven to be good recruitment sources for you?

    A.

    B.

    C.

8. What techniques for volunteer recognition have proven effective for you?

    A.

    B.

    C.

9. What is your own biggest problem/barrier to doing your job of working with volunteers?

10. What additional help from the National Guard would you like to see?

11. What ways (if any) do you utilize volunteers in helping you operate the volunteer management system for your Family Program?

FIGURE 5-1 — p. 2

12   If you were attending a training session on volunteer management, what three areas would you most like to see addressed?

❑ Planning a volunteer progarm ❑ Trends and issues in volunteering
❑ Innovative volunteer jobs ❑ Gaining support of park staff
❑ Recruitment ❑ Dealing with problem volunteers
❑ Screening & placement ❑ Recognition
❑ Training ❑ Supervising volunteers
❑ Gaining adminstrative support ❑ Exemplary family programs
❑ Marketing government volunteer programs to the community
❑ New roles for the Family Support program

❑ Other:_____

13. Are there any other specific concerns or questions that you would like to see addressed in the volunteer management training?

14. Please describe your total level of experience in managing volunteers in the Family Program or in other volunteer projects:

❑ Less than 6 months ❑ 6 months to 1 year
❑ 1 to 5 years experience ❑ 5 to 10 years experience
❑ Over 10 years experience

Please return the completed survey by August 15 to:
VM Systems
1807 Prairie
Downers Grove, IL 60515

FAX: 708/964-0841

Thank you.

FIGURE 5-1 — p. 3

SAMPLE SEMINAR EVALUATION SHEET

1. Please rate content of the seminar:

Excellent	Good	Poor
10	5	0

2. Please rate the usefullness of the seminar information:

Extremely Useful	Useful	Not at All
10	5	0

3. Please rate the presentation of materials:

Presented Extremely Well	Presented Adequately	Presented Poorly
10	5	0

4. Do you feel this information will help you be more effective in your job?

Yes	Moderately	No
10	5	0

5. How would you rate the presentor on clarity of information?

Extremely Clear	Clear	Not Clear
10	5	0

6. Did the presentation meet your need? ❏ yes ❏ no ❏ somewhat
   Please explain if you checked 'no' or 'somewhat':

   _____

   _____

7. What are your general feelings in regard to:

   Information presented verbally: _____

   Handouts: _____

   Presentor: _____

FIGURE 5-2

WORKSHOP EVALUATION
WORKING WITH VOLUNTEERS

What knowledge/information/skills did you gain from this workshop?

What information/activities were the most useful?

PLEASE EVALUATE HOW ADEQUATE EACH OF THE FOLLOWING WAS BASED ON YOUR NEEDS, USING A SCALE OF 1 TO 5.
1 = POOR   5 = EXCELLENT

Amount of time allowed for the workshop   _____

Amount of time allowed for questions/answers/discussion   _____

Quality of instruction   _____

Quality of information presented   _____

Overall quality of the workshop   _____

ADDITIONAL COMMENTS AND SUGGESTIONS:

Providing your name and title is optional:

NAME _____

TITLE _____

ADDRESS _____

FIGURE 5-3

END OF SESSION REACTION FORM

1. Did you find this workshop meaningful?

   Very much ☐   Quite a bit ☐   Some, but not much ☐   Very little ☐

2. Did you learn any new facts or get any new ideas that would be helpful on your job?

   Certainly did ☐   Probably did ☐   Maybe ☐   Not at all ☐

3. Was there enough opportunity for participation?

   Too much ☐   All that was
   needed ☐   Should have
   been more ☐   Should have been
   much more ☐

4. What did you like best about this workshop?

5. What suggestions do you have for future workshops
   (content, techniques, materials, temp, etc.)?

   TITLE OF WORKSHOP: _____

   NAME OF PRESENTOR: _____

   DATE: _____

   NAME: _____
   　　　　　Optional

FIGURE 5-4

EVALUATION

Workshop/Session _____

Workshop Date _____

Presenter(s) _____

	EXCELLENT						POOR
1. The organization of the presentation was:	7	6	5	4	3	2	1
2. The objectives of the presentation were:	7	6	5	4	3	2	1
3. The work of the presenter(s) was:	7	6	5	4	3	2	1

	VERY INTERESTING						POOR
4. The activities/exercises were:	7	6	5	4	3	2	1
5. Overall, I consider this presentation:	7	6	5	4	3	2	1

	HIGH NEED						NO NEED
6. Do you feel a need for additional information about this topic:	7	6	5	4	3	2	1

Were your expectations for the workshop met? How? _____

_____

What information/activities were most helpful? _____

_____

General comments: _____

_____

_____

FIGURE 5-5

WORKING WITH PEOPLE IN MEETINGS

HOW THEY ACT	WHY	WHAT TO DO
 GRIPER	Has a pet peeve. Professional griper. Has legitimate complaint.	Point out we can't change policy here; problem is to operate as best we can under the system. Indicate you'll discuss the problem with him privately later. Have a member of the group answer him. Indicate the pressures of time.
 WON'T TALK	Bored. Indifferent. Feels superior. Timid. Insecure.	Your actions will depend upon what is motivating him. Arouse his interest by asking for his opinion. Draw out the fellow next to him, then ask the quiet man to tell the fellow next to him what he thinks of the view expressed. If he is seated near you, ask his opinion so that he'll feel he is talking to you, not the group. If he is the "superior" type, ask for his view after indicating the respect held for experience. (Don't overdo this. The group will resent it.) Iritate him for a moment by tossing a provacative query. If the sensitive person won't talk, compliment him the first time he does. Be sincere!

FIGURE 5-6 — p.1

HOW THEY ACT	WHY	WHAT TO DO
RAMBLER	Talks about everything except the subject. Uses farfetched analogies and gets lost.	When he stops for breath, thank him, refocus his attention by restating the relevant points, and move on. Grin, tell him his point is interesting, point to the blackboard and in a friendly manner indicate we are a bit off the subject. Last resort: Glance at your watch.
PERSONALITY CLASH	Two or more members clash. Can divide your group into factions.	Emphasize points of agreements, minimize points of disagreement (If possible). Draw attention to objectives. Cut across with direct question on the topic. Bring a sound member into the discussion. Frankly ask that personalities be omitted.
WON'T BUDGE	Prejudiced. Hasn't seen your points.	Throw his view to the group, have group members straighten him out. Tell him that time is short and that you will be glad to discuss his point later. Ask him to accept the group viewpoint for the moment.
WRONG SUBJECT	Not rambling, just off base.	Take the blame: "Something I said must have led you off the subject; this is what we should be discussing." Restate the point or use the board.

FIGURE 5-6 — p. 2

HOW THEY ACT	WHY	WHAT TO DO
SIDE CONVERSATION	May be related to the subject. May be personal. Distracts members of the group and you.	Don't embarass them. Call one by name, ask him an easy question, or call one by name, then restate last opinion expressed or last remark made by group, and ask his opinion of it. If, during conference, you are in the habit of moving around the room, saunter and stand casually behind members who are talking. This should not be made obvious to the group.
INARTICULATE	Lacks ability to put thoughts in proper words. He is getting ideas but can't convey it. He needs help.	Don't say, "What you mean is this." Say, "let me repeat that" (then put it in better language).
DEFINATELY WRONG	Member comes up with a comment that is obviously incorrect.	Say, "I can see how you feel" or "That's one way of looking at it." Say, "I see your point, but can we reconcile that with the. . ."
SEARCHING FOR YOUR OPINION	Trying to put you on the spot. Trying to have you support one view. May be simply looking for your advice.	Generally, you should avoid solving their problems for them. Never take sides. Point out that your view is relatively unimportant, compared to the view of the people at the meeting. Don't let this become a phobia. There are times when you must and should give a direct answer. Before you do so, try to determine their reason for asking your view. Say, "First, let's get some other opinions." or "How do you look upon this point?" (select a member to reply).

FIGURE 5-6 — p. 3

HOW THEY ACT	WHY	WHAT TO DO
OVERLY TALKATIVE	He may be an "eager beaver" or a showoff. He may also be exceptionally well informed and anxious to show it, or just naturally wordy.	Don't be embarrassing or sarcastic . . . you may need his traits later on. Slow him down with some difficult questions. Interrupt with: "That's an interesting point . . . now let's see what the group thinks of it." In general, let the group take care of him as much as possible.
HIGH ARGUMENTATIVE	Combat personality . . . professional heckler May be normally good natured but upset by personal or job problems.	Keep your own temper firmly in check . . . don't let group get excited either. Honestly try to find merit in one of his points . . . express your agreement (or get the group to do so) . . . then move on to something else. When he makes an obvious misstatement, toss it to the group . . . let them turn it down. As a last resort, talk to him privately during a recess . . . try to find out what's bothering him . . . see if you can win his cooperation.
QUICKLY HELPFUL	Really trying to help, actually makes it difficult and keeps others out.	Cut across her tactfully by questioning others. Thank her, suggest "we put others to work." Use her for summerizing.

FIGURE 5-6 — p. 4

NOTES ON DEALING WITH
PROBLEM PEOPLE IN GROUP SETTING

Summary by: Cindy Swindell

From article entitled, *Leadership Techniques* (taken from *Manual for Small Meetings*, Bill Communications, Inc., 1975, Philadelphia, PA 19102, pp. 1-7).

CAUTION: Never get drawn into controversy (as leader) with any group members. Don't embarass, intimidate, argue with any participant — regardless.

1. **SILENT SAM:** shy, but may have lot to contribute, drawn out without being obvious, call on by name — ask direct, easy questions, have relate his experiences with the subject.

2. **ARGUING ALBERT:** always arguing, even over trivial points. **Don't** argue with. Turn arguments back to whole group for discussion.

3. **TALKER TIM:** something to say about everything, want to slow down but not shut off totally, (i.e.: control). Direct questions to others by name, interrupt to summarize when T.T. takes breath and ask for another's opinion —or— avoid looking at him. (catching his eye gives him his okay to start!)

4. **FLATTERER FRED:** continually agreeing with you and seeking your approval. This is false feedback from group. Bypass when possible. When seeking group feedback — call on more objective persons.

5. **WANDERING WILBURT:** sidetracks discussion with extraneous comments, opinions. Kindly thank; then throw a question to whole group which puts discussion back oncourse. If persists — weigh your desire to be kind against the damage being done to the discussion.

6. **BORED BILLY:** seems bored by the whole thing. It's your function to arouse interest — ask directly for his/her opinion or refer to B.B.'s specific experience of the topic.

7. **GRIPPING GUS:** whiney, complaining — often not legitimate. If complaint relates to topic — ask group to respond to G.G. If irrelevant, offer to discuss privately later. **Don't** dismiss person or the complaint.

8. **HECKLING HARRY:** "devils advocate" type; enjoys a good argument; likes the attention it brings. If argument gets personal — cut off right away. Debate can add to discussion — keep control of group, remain calm.

9. **SUPERIOR SAM:** knows all answers; discussion is waste of time because S.S. thinks answer is obvious. Others may feel foolish/resentful. Therefore, keep him "busy" — ask S.S.'s opinion or get him writing at the blackboard, for example.

FIGURE 5-7

HANDLING CONFLICT IN TRAINING GROUPS

Paul Friedman & Elaine Yarbrough
"Training Strategies from Start to Finish"
(Englewood-Cliffs: Prentice Hall, 1985)

Diagnosing	**Responding**

1. Assessing goals of conflicts
    • Content
    • Relational
	1. Divide means of reaching goals from needs people are trying to satisfy.
	2. Be aware of range of human needs (affection, control, inclusion).
	3. Listen for intensity of communication to decipher needs.
	4. Listen for repeated patterns of communication.
	5. Listen for incongruities in patterns of communication.
	6. Stay in touch with others and self in conflict by paraphrasing and breathing.

2. Assessing strategies to use	Strategic choices include: 1. Avoidance 2. Escalation 3. Maintenance 4. De-escalation

3. Typical conflict issues in training groups
    (a) Authority conflict:
      • Dependence
 	
      • Counterdependence
	1. Escalate conflict by being a catalyst
	    • Pick a fight
	    • Rigidify instructions
	    • Construct time for activities
	2. De-escalate conflict
	    • Wait and do not respond
	    • Use humor
	    • Alter-ego participants (speak the unspoken message)
	    • Discuss the interaction
	    • Ask for further information
	    • Coopt participants
	3. Escalate/de-escalate
	    • Dissipation – let the monopolizer continue at length
	    • Diversion – seek others' opinions
	    • Dramatization – mirror peoples' styles with humor
	    • Give people what they need – recognition, influence, etc.
	4. Avoidance
	    • Physical avoidance
	    • Put counterdependents together
	5. Maintenance
	    • Agree on how conflict will be handled
	    • Voice hidden concerns

FIGURE 5-8 — p. 1

(b) Conflicts around sex differences
  • Discrimination around fees
  • Sexual (flirting) responses

  • Differential treatment of male and female trainers (interruptions, etc.)
  • Put-downs of female through language, jokes, etc.

  • Put-down of males through sexist accusations, in-jokes, anger.

1. Directly clarify fees
2. Ignore the response
3. Divert them through humor
4. Talk frankly about them
5. Be aware of sexual signs you may be sending out
6. Male/female modeling of peer communication
7. Have male direct the interaction to the female
8. Use humor
9. Reverse roles
10. Use more dominate behaviors
11. Clarify your goals
12. Understand women's perceptions of professional roles
13. Clarify communication around sex roles
14. Re-empower participants by letting them take the lead and give feedback about sexist behavior

(c) Conflicts arising through communication games
  • To prove others are not OK

  • To prove self is not OK

1. Provide positive recognition of self and others
2. Refuse to counterblame and put others down
3. Communicate congruently
4. Provide feedback on games

FIGURE 5-8 — p. 2

IF IT WEREN'T FOR THEM
Tips for the Seminar Leader

Group leaders need to know how to handle all sorts of personality types. Two training experts explain how to keep your poise no matter who is in your group.

By Kevin Montgomery and Dorothy M. Neddermeyer

As a nonprofit executive, you may well be required to serve as a seminar or workshop leader. And you may discover, as many have before you, that one of your biggest problems is dealing with the distracting personality of one or more of your participants.

It seems that at almost every workshop or seminar there is at least one "difficult" person. His or her personality tends to hinder the learning process and distract the group leader from the prescribed goals.

If group leaders feel that the distracting behavior is a result of their style of leadership, they may feel inadquate or frustrated. It is important, therefore, that they understand that these personalities are usually enduring styles rather than transient behaviors exhibited as a result of the group process.

In working with numerous human relations training groups, we have isolated a variety of personality styles. As with life in general, it is the exception that rivets our attention and stimulates reflection. Using Eric Berne's *Games People Play* as our paradigm, we have abstracted five distracting personality styles that appear consistently in our groups. They may be identified as follows:

1. Yes, but
2. Wooden leg
3. If it weren't for them (the boss, co-workers, management, etc.)
4. Ain't it awful
5. Now I've got you, you S.O.B.

While each of these styles is characterized by different behaviors, a common trait is avoidance behavior. Each style serves the purpose of avoiding becoming involved in the learning process and/or having to consider seriously the issues being raised.

Our experience, working in various settings, reveals that every organization's employees manifest these personality styles in varying degrees. Organizations with no competitors have minimal influence from external forces to prompt growth, a situation which promotes organizational stagnation. This stagnation finds indirect expression through all the communication channels in the system and has its terminal impact on the attitude of the indiividual employee. Somehow, maintaining the status quo becomes both an organizational and personal dictum. When confronted in a human relations training program by information that has a high probability of generating cognitive dissonance, the individual "instinctively" wants to put his or her head in the sand or fight to defend the status quo. This syndrom is manifested behaviorally as the "games" we have identified.

The following compendium represents a synthesis that we have developed to aid group leaders in successfully managing various personality styles and in promoting effective learning.

One person does not have the right to ruin an otherwise well-functioning group. But one person can do just that if you don't know how to respond to him or her. As you practice the responses given here, you will become more and more adept both at identifying different personality types and responding to them effectively. Instead of watching helplessly as all your well-laid plans go awry, you will have the satisfaction of knowing that *you* are in control.

FIGURE 5-9 — p. 1

PERSONALITY STYLES

Symptoms	Reasons	What to do
1. YES BUT Member presents problem regarding work situation. Other members and/or leader present possible solution: "Have you considered . . .?" Member responds, "Yes, but . . ."	Member seeks no solution to problem. Desires to remain in the same dilemma. Doesn't want change. Wants to make others appear inferior by rejecting their solutions as not quite good enough.	After second response of "Yes, but," if circumstances and skills of group leader permit, use gentle confrontation to redirect the energy and focus of the member. Ask, for instance, "What is it you want to accomplish?" Or point out, "It is important to consider solutions before you reject them." If member insists there is no solution, suggest the need to learn ways to cope and cease complaining. OR If circumstances and skill of group leader do not permit confrontation, after the second response of "Yes, but," intercede politely and ask another member a different question.
2. WOODEN LEG Member makes statements of helplessness: "I can't do . . .," "I'll try . . .," "You expect too much," "I'm not sure I can change at my age," and so on.	Member feels generally inadequate. Wants group either to rescue or feel sorry for him or her (poor defenseless me).	Encourage him or her to re-evaluate. Ask, "Do you want to . . .?" The appropriate response is, "Yes, I do," or, "No, I don't." If the member continues to play "wooden leg," intercede politely and ask another member a different question.
3. IF IT WEREN'T FOR THEM (THE BOSS, CO-WORKERS, MANAGEMENT) Member makes statements blaming others.	Member doesn't take responsibility for own behavior or solutions to conflict. Blames others for problems, inadequacies, etc.	Use questions to bring out others aspects. Ask, for example, "Have you discussed the issue with those involved?" or, "Have you told those involved how you feel?" or, "Have you shared your ideas and opinions?" Encourage member to look at the situation from others' perspectives.
4. AIN'T IT AWFUL Member relates "war stories" regarding organization's policies with no apparent purpose in mind.	Member wants to elicit sympathy from others. "Ain't it awful, I have it so bad here." Member wants to look superior by airing others' faults, thus avoiding a recognition of how she or he is part of the problem and a responsibility for the resolution (i.d., innocent victim).	Empathize with member's situation, but avoid joining in the game of "ain't it awful." Ask member what she or he does to change the situation. If member seeks to find solution, engage in problem-solving dialogue. If member switches to "wooden-leg," empathize and refer to wooden leg dialogue (see no. 2 above).
5. NOW I'VE GOT YOU, YOU S.O.B. Member looks for and points out issues to discredit the information and the leader's ability: "Have you worked in public relations, fundraising, direct mail, etc.? Unless you have, you can't say this works." "How much time have you spent out in the field?" "What is your background?"	Member is threatened by new information. Is unable to accept different and possibly easier ways of doing something. Feels inadequate and unable to change. Fears change.	Avoid becoming embroiled in answering a series of questions about your background. Empathize with member's fear of change. Encourage members to discuss feelings regarding change and how they see themselves as change agents. Remember that fear often precipitates aggressive, obstinate behavior. Keep your temper; the members are not attacking you. Empathize with their actions to the context.

NON PROFIT WORLD REPORT
May/June 1984

FIGURE 5-9 — p. 2

CHAPTER 6

TRAINER'S TOOLS

The tools a trainer uses must become an enhancement, rather than a detractor, in the learning process. Listed here are some commonly used and readily available tools of our trade. They range from AV equipment to room arrangements, handouts to quotes, and should reflect your passion for quality and attention to learner's needs. Use them all wisely, smoothly and well.

VISUALS

Every been to a training where someone used charts and overheads **so effectively** that they made the workshop content come to life for you?

Ever been to a workshop where the charts and overheads were **so poor** that they detracted from the content and frustrated you to death?

Welcome to the wonderful world of visuals!

Visuals of any kind — overheads, handouts, graphs, flip charts, signs, etc., can add a tremendous depth to a training and assist the visual learner IF they are well planned and executed.

GUIDELINES

For any kind of visual, certain guidelines prevail:

1. **Know your audience** — who are they? what roles do they play? what might best help them learn? what is their level of competence? what symbolizes validity for them?

2. **What is your goal for the presentation?** simply to give information? change? problem solving? decision making? relationship building?

3. **Have enough time** — too much or too little can ruin any training — complex visuals whipped away in 30 seconds or ones left on the screen for 15 minutes can frustrate audiences and become a BLOCK to learning rather than an AIDE.

4. **Know and control the physical setting** — arrange appropriate lighting, backgrounds, seating for optimum viewing.

5. **Where do visuals enhance learning** — plan your content floor with visuals as an integral part. Know when they are an absolute must and when they could be eliminated if necessary. Key your visuals in your notes. (I use a little symbol drawn in red for flip chart use 🖼 , overhead 🖼 , and handouts 🖼 . The symbols are easy to spot as I glance at notes.)

6. **Put careful thought and time into the creation** of visuals and modify them as needed after being tested with audiences.

7. **Condense information**, use symbols and abbreviations, eliminate unnecessary words or figures.

8. **Design visuals** to be viewed by a whole audience cleanly and insure that people in the back row can read them.

GRAPHIC OPTIONS

There are many options open to you as you design supplementary visual materials to reinforce and support your training. A partial list of the most commonly chosen ones follows along with characteristics, design tips, etc.

A. **CHARTS**

1. Most **universally used** — very available — flexible.

2. **Inexpensive** to reproduce.

3. **Easy to brighten up** (color, cartoons, etc.).

4. Preparation

    a. Use thin card or illustration board — opaque, durable, available in colors, professional appearance, large.

    b. Keep simple and uncluttered.

    c. Keep words limited to 3-7 per line; 7-8 lines per chart (10 maximum).

    d. Keep copy high on chart for maximum visibility from back of room. Leave deep margin on bottom.

    e. Add color and cartoons to enhance.

B. FLIP CHARTS

1. **Flexible use** as you work through your presentation.

    a. Good place for capturing audience response (you may need to ask audience volunteers to help record responses).

    b. Can be prepared ahead of time — do in sequence on tablet — mark or tab corners for ease in location. I use sticky note paper at bottom left of predrawn pages with key word to remind me of what is drawn there.

2. **Limit** to ten **lines** of 2" high letters, 1/4 inch thick (magic marker size) if it is to be read at back of a room holding 200 people. One to three lines are best for focusing in on main concepts. Do not make letters less than one inch high for groups up to 50.

3. **Keep style of lettering and color similar** except when you want to emphasize key points. I alternate colors back and forth when moving through sequential lists to help the viewer keep their eye on the correct line.

4. **Use with smaller audiences** — up to 25 — if much to be written on it.

C. OVERHEADS

1. **Requires knowledge** of how to use overhead project.

    a. Know how to turn on/off easily.

    b. Tape power cord to floor so you don't trip.

    c. Test it for proper distance from screen before workshop.

    d. Have spare bulb available.

    e. Clean off lens and glass top before training.

    f. Do not place it so that you have to walk in front of it while it's projecting.

    g. Place screen carefully so that all can see — avoid light directly overhead or behind screen — try to place it where room lights do not have to be turned off to use it.

2. **Can use portions of the transparency** by covering points, then advancing from point to point by moving covering.

3. **Colors** greatly **enhance** transparencies — cartoons too (see chart, Figures 6-1, 6-2, pp. 137-138).

4. Use pointer to **draw attention** to one part of transparency — point to screen or visual on projector.

5. **Can add overlays** to transparencies to build a concept or progressive instruction.

6. Use in **larger (50) audiences** — the bigger the audience the bigger the print must be. (Rather than reinventing the wheel of specific instructions on how to prepare and use transparencies, I'll simply refer you here to Figures 6-3, 6-4, 6-5, and 6-6, pp. 139-142. Marvelous handouts prepared by trainer Andy Hart of Littleton, Colorado, who helps people in workshops learn the art of overhead projectors.)

7. Prevent overheads from slipping on the projector or each other if you're "building" a visual for an audience by touching each with a wet finger.

D. CHALK BOARD

1. May be limited in size but can be erased to **add new information.**

2. Use of colored chalk can enhance learning.

3. **Print carefully** — try to maintain straight lines.

4. Can be **used for key points** you wish to return to again and again.

5. Use for smaller audiences if much is to be written.

E. VELCRO OR FELT BOARDS

1. Seem to see me coming and refuse to hold pieces in place, but you may have better luck than I.

2. Great for **progressive learning** steps or building a visual (i.e.: pie chart, etc.).

3. Must be **handled very smoothly** or it detracts as you add pieces.

4. Use with audiences up to 25 people.

F. SLIDES

1. Used when photos add to presentation.

2. Help **tell a story.**

3. **Requires competence** of user plus knowledge of equipment to allow trainer to use effectively.

4. **Check** slides and equipment out **CAREFULLY** (one upside down slide can ruin an entire presentation).

5. Can give very **professional** high tone flavor to training if done well.

6. Requires some **room darkening**.

7. Must use smoothly — **practice, practice, practice!**

8. If used with sound, make sure it's **synchronized**.

G. MOVIES OR VIDEO TAPES

1. Be very **familiar** with equipment or have expert on hand to operate.

2. **Preview** all films entirely before using — if you use one with many audiences, rethink its appropriateness for each audience PRIOR to use. Check for even the slightest detail that might offend an audience, i.e.: no minority representation, prejudices, etc., etc.

3. Video screens are not good for large audiences — too **small** and hard to see.

4. **Demands darkness** in room — know where the light switches are!

5. Can be very **impressive** to audiences and nice break for all.

6. Movies can be used with very **large** audiences; video tapes — can use rule of thumb of one person per inch of TV monitor (i.e.: 25" screen to 25 trainees).

FIRST AID FOR VISUALS

Billie Ann Myers, the Director of the Arkansas Division of Volunteerism, is, like this author, an ex-art teacher. She offers a wonderful workshop designed to convince attendees that they can indeed create and spruce up visuals even without a degree in art!

Some simple ways to offer visuals first aid that Myers suggests, include:

1. Add a border.

2. Add a picture.

3. Cut wording to key ideas only.

4. Add boldness (weight) to lettering.

5. Use color for emphasis.

6. Use columns or sectioning.

7. Add graphic devices such as bullets, stars, etc.

8. Ink twice for darker colors.

9. Put picture on top, headline under picture and text under headline.

10. Abbreviate long words to save space.

11. Make all drawings **BOLD** — avoid thin-lined words and pictures.

COLOR   Rule of thumb — USE IT!

Color enhances attention so apply it cleverly. Don't automatically grab the black marker. Use bold colors — don't be afraid of them. Underline key words in color when emphasizing a point.

In Figures 6-1 and 6-2, pp. 137-138, you will see Myers and Hart's outlines of how colors can be used effectively.

TIPS   Some color tips to use:

1. Black and yellow are the easiest for the eye to see — red and white next easiest (now you understand why road signs are printed the way they are!).

2. Blue, black, red, and green are easy to see on white or tan flip chart paper.

3. Avoid yellow chalk on green board — it's hard to see from far away — use white. Do not use red unless it's in a bullet — red letters on green cause the eye to fade back and forth.

4. Go over a color more than once to make it intense — it will draw more attention that way.

5. Don't worry about colors "clashing" — all colors can go together.

6. Dark colors can go over lighter ones — but not the reverse.

7. There are five color combinations the eye sees as pleasing:

   a. Monochromatic — one color and its variations plus black and white.

   b. Analogous — colors adjacent to each other on the color wheel (see Figure 6-1) they project harmony.

   c. Complimentary — opposite each other on the color wheel (see Figure 6-1) they excite viewers.

   d. Triad — 3 colors equidistant on the color wheel, (see Figure 6-1) they create interest.

   e. Split complementary — a color and the two colors on either side of its complement (red, plus yellow green, plus blue green).

As an ex-art teacher myself, let me just add a few tips on the use of visuals:

1. Practice until you're comfortable with them — remember they are there to ENHANCE the learning, not provide a diversion that detracts as the trainer fumbles for switches, misplaces transparencies, forgets how to make equipment work or finds they only brought a yellow marker for the flip chart.

2. Have professionals help in design if you don't have a natural sense for it.

3. Bigger is better is the rule of thumb of printing — make sure the width of your letters is in proportion to height.

G IS BAD, **G** IS MUCH BETTER!

4. Take your time; print or write clearly:

5. Decide what to EMPHASIZE then consider using color, bolder or varied printing, border or an underline to do so.

6. Avoid yellow or pastel lettering — it's hard to read.

7. Permanent markers bleed through flip chart paper — water color markers are better (and don't smell).

8. If you have some art talent, use it. I have become known for some cartooning I use in presentations — it helps people remember information and is unique . . . breaks up long stretches of learning.

9. Practice lettering styles till you can do them easily — you don't need to know more than a few to jazz up your visuals:

·Visuals· ·Visuals· ·Visuals· VISUALS·

10. Use symbols when you can.

11. Boxes and borders help categorize information.

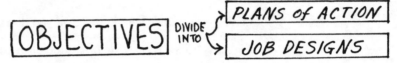

12. Use columns and bullets to break up information.

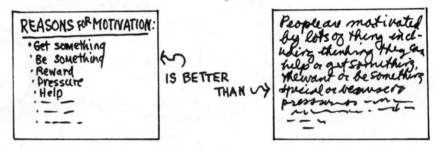

13. When all else fails, use the happy face.

14. If you can draw a W, H, O, U or V you can draw any stick figure:

15. Use graphics to show data when possible.

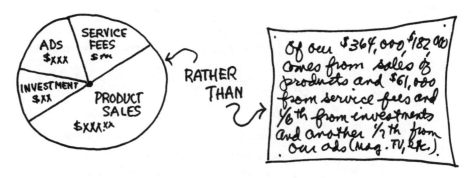

especially comparisons:

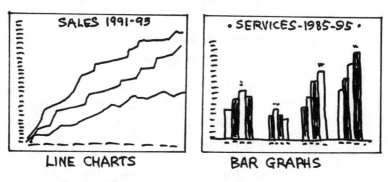

16. Try to keep balanced.

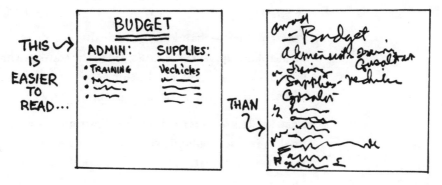

17. If you feel like all thumbs when it comes to drawing, clip art (pre-drawn art work you can use without copyright infringement) is available at art supply stores, office supply houses or through catalogs.

18. When doing a set of handouts, you may want to locate a clip art cartoon character in many poses and use them to tie all your pieces together.

HANDOUTS

Handouts are the written information you give to participants to compliment, enhance, expand or support your training.

They can offer additional information such as:

1. **Reinforce key points of training** — use in outline form for ease of reading; helps the visual learner by being able to **see** the information they have heard; assists the auditory learner who can concentrate on what you're saying and not have to break concentration by stopping to take notes.

2. **Greater in-depth information** — use to offer greater information on a particular point in your training; excellent way to provide technical or research data; footnote carefully. Use when you have a limited time in which to train a complex subject.

3. **Additional information** — use when training in a broad subject (i.e.: fund-raising, legislation, marketing, etc.) for which you then offer examples of the concept being trained. Can expand learning of participants.

4. **Bibliography** — a handout that can be invaluable to participants who want more information; if it covers several subjects, list references by category.

5. **Participatory** — handouts participants use either during the training or in follow-up: surveys, tests, fill-in-the-blanks, worksheets, etc.; have the instructions listed step-by-step at top of handouts to reinforce your verbal instructions; allow enough time for use.

6. **Case studies** — offer stories that illustrate a learning concept; may be used in problem solving, skill development or practice to aide trainees in putting information to use; a practical application option to compliment training.

In designing handouts, label them carefully and use the same principles you use for visuals. Have them printed or typed carefully.

COPYRIGHT   Add your name and copyright symbol plus date by year at the bottom of each of your unique handouts. These then become your legal property and will hopefully deter people from using them without your OK. (If you are an independent trainer, they also service as a continuing marketing ad for you and your training product. You may even want to add your address so interested people can contact you.)

When quoting any other source or adapting information from others, credit them carefully. You are allowed to quote up to 100 words without getting written permission from the source, but always use quote marks and credit lines to denote someone elses work.

FILE

Update your handouts frequently — review the data and visuals so that they are not "dated." Your audience deserves the best and latest information possible.

I keep a master note book with a copy, organized by subject in alphabetical order, of every handout I've ever created or used for reference. Sometimes a handout you used years ago but then forgot about may help you as you design a new one for a particular training.

CLIP ART

Consider creating a clip art and design folder of things you see that you might incorporate into your own handouts. Art work in phone book yellow pages, newspapers, advertisements, greeting cards, etc., can be clipped and saved in your file as well as items that have a catchy design you might like to use.

USE

Decide ahead of time how you want to use your handouts. I ask that mine all be given to participants as they arrive and I give instructions **not** to staple them together so they can be used at random.

Others prefer to have them given out as they come to a particular point in the training — the dribble effect I call it — so that they do not have people reading over material before it's offered verbally.

However you offer handouts, tell folks how you plan to have them used so they won't be wondering. You might say "The handouts cover the key points of the topic and offer further reading on the subject — you can use them to take notes now or set them aside for use later." The idea is to remove any questions (and even occasionally, anxiety) about how participants will be expected to interact with the material.

Handouts are a valuable part of any training and can enhance understanding and learning for trainees. Consider and create them carefully — they can add credibility and expansion to any training subject.

ROOM ARRANGEMENTS

How a training room is set up can be a critical factor in the success of the learning. Choose the style carefully and in accordance with the needs the participants have during the session.

The most common set-ups used are:

CONFERENCE

1. **Conference Style** — Gives participants both tables and chairs; used with smaller groups; variations include:

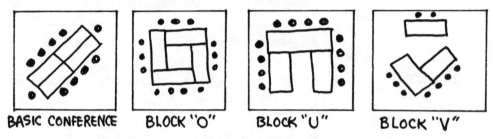

BASIC CONFERENCE   BLOCK "O"   BLOCK "U"   BLOCK "V"

WORKSHOP

2. **Workshop Style** — Gives participants tables and chairs, arranged so larger numbers of people can see leader's table and training space; variations include:

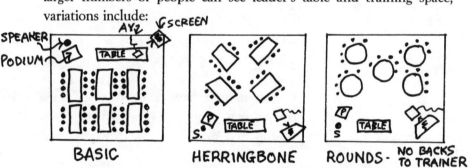

BASIC   HERRINGBONE   ROUNDS - NO BACKS TO TRAINER

CLASSROOM

3. **Classroom Style** — Tables and chairs can both be available but set up for large groups facing toward trainer's area:

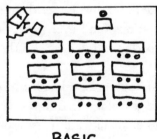

BASIC

THEATRE

4. **Theatre Style** — For very large groups, no tables:

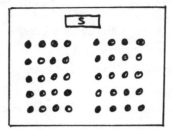

BANQUET

5 **Banquet Style** — Lots of people packed in with both tables and chairs; used mostly for meal functions with speakers; variations include:

BANQUET "E"   BANQUET SINGLES   ROUND TABLES · SOME BACKS TO HEAD TABLE

Choose your room set-up in accordance with the climate you wish to promote: intimacy; sharing; formality; speaker-focused; interactive participation; technical; relaxed; formal/informal; etc.

Think of your room as the framework of the training event — it must be appropriate without being overpowering and enhance, rather than detract, from the learning.

THE TRAINER'S SURVIVAL KIT

Most trainer's have learned to have a survival kit at the ready so they can be prepared in almost any eventuality. If you plan to be a traveling trainer hopping airplanes from town to town, you will want to ask your hosts to insure some of these items are at the training site . . . that way you'll have less "stuff" to carry around and the airlines of the world won't have to figure out how to store it before takeoffs!

1. **Handouts** — Even though you sent your masters to the host for reproduction, it's a good idea to take a complete set along in case any got misplaced.

2. **Extension Cord** — Always count on the need to place the projector 25 inches out of reach of the nearest outlet! It's a given.

3. **Easel For Flip Chart Paper** — If you do your training with one program or in one general location, you might want to invest in a good

sturdy one that won't tip over when you try to write on the paper or collapse as you're about to unveil your best graphic.

4. **Markers** — Invest in a good set. Avoid permanent markers that you can smell three buildings away (they also bleed through several layers of paper). Water color markers now come in vibrant colors — have at least six. If you will be asking trainees to do brainstorming and record it, provide dark markers for them too.

5. **Paper and Pencils** — Someone always needs them!

6. **Name Tags or Tents** — Some way to identify participants that allows you and others to communicate. Have names printed in large print. (As I grow older, I've thought seriously about introducing a new constitutional amendment that says all name tags should be printed in 2-inch high letters and back-lighted, but decided that might be a little pushy.)

7. **Masking Tape** — Count on it! Something will need to be taped, masked or patched before the training ends!

8. **Spare Projector Bulb** — I've never needed one when a spare one was available — only when one couldn't be found. Murphy's Law strikes again.

9. **Travel Alarm Clock** — Don't assume you'll have a working clock within sight in every training room . . . or that one that is there is: (1) in plain sight (I've had several <u>behind</u> me), (2) in working order. The only danger is leaving them on the podium. I've left them four times in twelve years which leads to my sub-point: Buy cheap ones and develop <u>NO</u> sentimental attachment!

10. **Extra Overhead Transparencies** — You never know when the afternoon speaker will come down with poison ivy. Be prepared to fill in.

A WORD ABOUT TAKING CARE OF YOU

In my newsletter for trainers, *Training Wheels,* I have frequently addressed the issue of need for self-care by a trainer. When examining the subject of training tools, we need to include those "softer" areas that can help you take care of you!

Training is hard work. When done well, it looks like the duck who is gliding over the water smoothly but is really paddling like crazy underneath!

It is physically draining as you work on your feet for up to eight hours a day — bouncing from lectern to projector to small groups needing help and back to the lectern again.

It taxes your legs, back and voice as you work to project words and enthusiasm to the back row. It taxes your brain as you juggle ten considerations at once as you work to transfer what is in your head to the participants.

While everyone else "breaks," you are bombarded by people wanting a minute of your time and a word of advise on a usually thorny problem. During meals you pick at a salad while others pick your brain.

When people get sluggish after lunch, you (who would <u>love</u> just 15 minutes of a "feet-up/head-down" nap) must pump up the adrenalin to keep everyone awake and involved.

When the workshop is over, folks glide out after just "one more question" to you or request for a quick-fix to a problem, leaving you to gather all your notes, repack the AV equipment, flip chart and screen, round up the markers, leftover handouts, your podium clock, extension cord, masking tape and try to mash much of this into your bulging briefcase.

Then it's off to an airport, motel or home where more demands can lurk, plus the promise of more training the next day or soon thereafter.

After such a description, you're probably wondering if this is my subtle way of discouraging you — NO — quite to the contrary, it is my not-subtle-at-all way of equipping you with the reality of training. To let you think it's all spotlight and glitter, roses and accolades, trophies and honors would be to set you up for unrealistic expectations and hollow promises.

Training <u>is</u> hard work and like anything else, therein lies it's reward, because when done well and carefully with the learner and his/her learning as the goal, great rewards are in store for you. Rewards of personal satisfaction in knowing:

1. You helped people grow.

2. You helped them be more effective.

3. You made a difference.

. . . And if you keep it all in perspective, you even had FUN along the way.

Taking care of you must, however, be a continuing priority as you race around saving the world from ignorance and misperception. I would urge you to take the time to read *How To Take Care of You . . . So You Can Take Care of Others,* a book I wrote after ignoring physical warning signs and landing in the critical care section of my local hospital. It can give you an in-depth look at the wellness issue.

SELF-CARE TOOLS & TIPS

For our purposes here, however, I would simply ask you to consider the following quick-fix list of caregiving suggestions:

1. Create and tap a personal and professional support system which can afford you assistance, relief, fun and distraction as needed.

2. Check your body tension level as you train — keep muscles in back, neck, shoulders and jaw as relaxed as possible.

3. Sit down while trainees work in group assignments.

4. Don't feel obligated to accept every off-hour social invitation. If you're too tired to go out in the evening, say so by declining politely.

5. Order room service if you feel the need to avoid being interrupted over meals.

6. Wear comfortable clothing — especially as you travel.

7. Between training events, schedule time just for yourself. Do things that revive, relax and renew you.

8. Don't overbook your training calendar. Consider travel time needs.

9. Identify "playmates" who help you laugh and enjoy life.

10. Don't take yourself too seriously!

QUOTES

In my last two years of high school, I went to a small school in Washington, Illinois. While there, I developed two great life-long loves — classical music and quotations. Both can be attributed to my music teacher, Miss Francis Whittaker, who ignored my inability to read a note of music and insisted that one could still love good music aesthetically without knowing its technicalities.

Each week she placed a great quote on the blackboard. She made no reference to them; simply placed them there for us to absorb or ignore as we saw fit.

I loved them and was fascinated to see such wisdom on such a variety of subjects. From that time forward, and often to background music of Debussey and Chopin, I've collected quotes where ever I can find them.

It's become a challenge to uncover them in unlikely hiding places — cartoons, advertising, the yellow pages, music lyrics, children's stories and poetry — even bumper stickers and greeting cards. Of course, books, magazines and newspapers offer the greatest wealth of quotes, but even then I look for them in unusual works that offer gems tucked in off-beat topics.

In all my trainings I use quotes to illustrate points, open or close sessions or "spice up" some heavy topics. I have my favorites on 3x5 cards that I carry with me to all trainings, keeping them on the podium for handy use.

I urge you to start a file of quotes and keep it growing through the years. Don't worry if you'll ever "use" them all. The larger and broader your quote file, the more likely you are to find a use for each.

I share here some of my favorites. Thank you Miss "Whit"!

✦ *"There is a destiny that makes us brothers — none goes his way alone; All that we send into the lives of others, comes back into our own." Edwin Markam (I use it to end almost all my trainings. I got it from a Christmas card in the 1970's)*

✦ *"Many an open mind should be closed for repairs."*

✦ *"Denial is the alternative to change." Alice Sargent*

✦ *"It is necessary, therefore it is possible."*

✦ *"Refusal to learn is more deeply a refusal to do." Abraham Maslow*

✦ *"Complex problems of today call for new approaches based on collaboration and interdependence rather than on competition. The solutions require risk and experimentation and working out problems together. They require a partnership so that the parts of the system do not stale mate one another." Alice Sargent*

✦ *"The greatest use of life is to spend it for something that outlasts it." William James*

✦ *"Personally, I'm always ready to learn, although I do not always like being taught." Winston Churchill*

✦ *"Never try to teach a pig to sing. It wastes your time and annoys the pig."*

✦ *"Nothing is easier than fault finding, no talent, no self-denial, no brains, no character are required to set up in the grumbling business . . ." Robert West*

✦ *"The greatest good we can do for others is not just to share our riches with them . . . but to enable them to discover their own!" Sister Carita*

✦ *"The greatest revolution in our generation is that human beings, by changing the inner attitudes of their minds can change the outer aspects of their lives." William James*

✦ *"No one wanted to be the least. Then Jesus took a towel and basin and so redefined greatness." Richard Foster*

TIPS

Many of the following are found within the contents of this book, but bear repeating:

1. My overheads are my major notes.
2. Wear comfortable shoes.
3. Trust your instincts.
4. If you aren't sure . . . ask!
5. Laugh to relax yourself and the audience.
6. Don't take yourself too seriously.
7. Remember that not everyone comes to learn in a workshop.
8. Read evaluations when you can digest them positively.
9. Never eat heavily before or during trainings.
10. Never check your briefcase at airports.
11. Carry a master of your handouts in case your host lost them.
12. Carry more overheads then you can use in case you need to fill in for someone else.
13. Carry your letters of agreement, brochure, etc. to trainings.
14. Have lots of business cards in your pockets.
15. Have the home phone number of your client.
16. Know ahead of time what $$ demands you will have at a site. Carry credit cards and cash.
17. Find out and dress appropriately for the client.
18. Make your own flight arrangements.
19. READ, READ, READ . . . keep a clipping file on subjects.

20. Watch others training . . . get info and tips.

21. Team train only with people you know well.

22. Never believe your own press clippings.

23. Keep your bio up to date . . . stress actions not awards.

24. Never embarrass audiences or individuals.

25. Keep your language appropriate.

26. Keep water at podium with lemon in it if possible.

27. If you lose your place, relax, take a sip of water to give you a few seconds to regroup and go on.

28. Train like an athlete — being on your feet all day is physically demanding.

29. Don't be afraid to say "I don't know."

30. Avoid staying in people's homes who won't let you relax.

31. Avoid being scheduled breakfast through late night. That's all work, no rest!

32. Do not schedule training in high demand times (during moves, major change, holidays, etc.)

33. Avoid making people sit for more than 45 min. - 1 hr. if possible.

34. Get everything in writing from client as to expectations, etc.

35. Check out meanings behind words of client wanting to hire you.

36. Avoid power struggles.

37. Never play games.

38. Continually refresh yourself mentally, emotionally, spiritually and physically.

39. Schedule time off after a particularly hectic period of work.

40. Stay in tune with changing needs of organization or audiences.

41. Build a support system and use it.

42. Develop a hobby or activity that is counter-point to your training work.

43. Use relaxation techniques during long training sessions for yourself.

44. Stay flexible.

45. Learn from others.

46. Respect audiences' intelligence.

47. Be passionate on your topics . . . refine them constantly . . . be open to new ideas.

48. Believe in yourself . . . you offer a good product at a good price . . . like yourself.

49. Don't get hung up on other people's criticisms . . . adopt writer Jennifer James' definition of criticism as "verbal slugs" that are ugly, stick to you and suck your blood. Your own self worth comes from what you think of yourself . . . not what others think of you. Be emotionally independent, be kind to children, adults, seniors, pets, the earth and yourself. Understand that true success and worth lies not in what you DO as much as in who you ARE and how you RELATE to others.

Laugh alot,
    Take time to smell the flowers.
        Enjoy and Love
            Stay balanced
                and carry your overheads with you at all times!

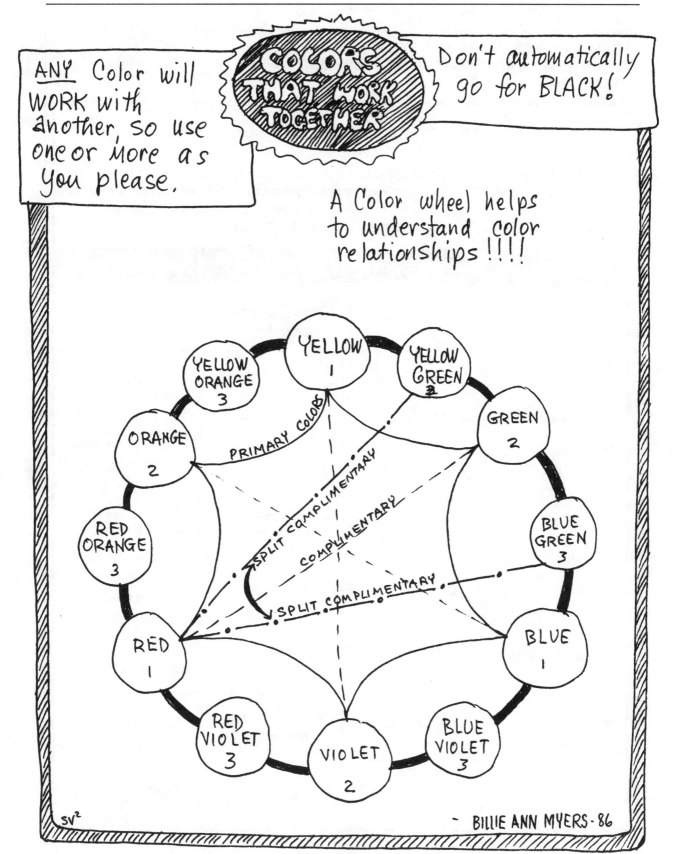

FIGURE 6-1

TRANSPARENCIES — TAMING THE TECHNOLOGY
VOLUNTEER MANAGEMENT PROFESSIONALS
ANDY HART

COLOR ASSOCIATIONS — EMOTIONAL RESPONSES

In this colorful world, black and white transparencies just don't make it. Color can be added to overheads by several methods, including the use of felt pens, color adhesive film, color write-on film, overlays and by chemical means. But what colors to use? 3-M suggests the following color associations and emotional responses.

COLOR	MENTAL ASSOCIATIONS	DIRECT ASSOCIATIONS	OBJECTIVE EXPRESSION
RED	Hot, Fire, Heat	Danger, Christmas, 4th of July	Passionate, Exciting, Fervid, Active
ORANGE	Warm, Metallic, Atumnal	Halloween Thanksgiving	Jovial, Lively Energetic, Forceful
YELLOW	Sunlight	Caution	Cheerful, Inspiring Vital, Celestial
GREEN	Cool, Nature, Water	Clear St. Patrick's Day	Quiet, Refreshsing, Peaceful, Nascent
BLUE	Cold, Sky, Water, Ice	Service, Flag	Subduing, Melancholy, Contemplative, Sober
PURPLE	Cool, Mist, Darkness, Shadow	Mourning, Easter	Dignified, Mournful, Mystic
WHITE	Cool, Snow	Cleanliness, Flag, Mother's Day	Pure, Clean, Frank
BLACK	Neutral, Night, Emptiness	Mourning	Funeral, Ominous, Depressing, Deadly

FIGURE 6-2

TRANSPARENCIES — TAMING THE TECHNOLOGY
VOLUNTEER MANAGEMENT PROFESSIONALS
ANDY HART

LAYOUT AND DESIGN

1. The primary function of an overhead transparency is to communicate. The most commonly made mistake is placing too much copy on it.

2. You can create an original on a layout sheet and transfer it to transparency film or make it directly on the film itself.

3. Keep your transparencies simple. Limit your copy to 6-8 words per line and the number of lines to 8-10. Simplify complex ideas and make into a series of transparencies rather than a single one.

4. Use easy to read lettering, not fancy curlicues and old english designs.

5. No lettering should be smaller than 1/4 inch.

6. Develop dominance and subordination of ideas through varying the size of the lettering. Points of equal value can be unified by using a symbol or asterisk before each of them.

7. The use of blue-line grid sheets with 1/4 inch squares as layout sheets makes it easier to keep letters uniform and straight.

8. Make room for a transparency frame by limiting the image area to 7-1/2" x 9". This is easily done by laying a frame over a grid sheet and in blue pencil tracing around the aperture. This visualizes the area which can be used.

9. The general rule is to place artwork no closer than 1/2 inch from the edge of the aperture. Placing it too close to the edge makes the transparency look too crowded.

10. Type and/or art should be carbon based (#2 pencil, carbon typewriter ribbon, printed material, etc.)

11. Mistakes must be erased or cut out completely on originals to be imaged in an infrared machine. Liquid or chalk cover-ups will work on originals to be imaged on plain paper copier film or to be duplicated before imaging in an infrared machine.

12. Use lines to draw attention.

13. Because screens are generally rectangular, vertical compositions can run off the top and the bottom of them. To compensate for this, the projector must be moved closer to the screen thereby reducing letter size and readability of the transparency.

14. Avoid vertical lettering. Because we've been taught to read left to right it hinders readability.

15. Use color to unify or highlight what you want the audience to see.

16. Use the rule of thirds when trying to decide where to place a drawing. Using a blue pencil divide the layout sheets into thirds both vertically and horizontally. Where the lines intersect is a good place to put a picture.

17. Vary the use of formal and informal balance when designing a set of transparencies.

FIGURE 6-3

TRANSPARENCIES — TAMING THE TECHNOLOGY
VOLUNTEER MANAGEMENT PROFESSIONALS
ANDY HART

TECHNIQUES

FRAMING

Eliminates light leaks around the edges of a transparency, assures that it will lie flat, and permits easier handling by the presenter. Notes and questions can be written on the edges of the frame. Framed transparencies are easier to store.

—Lay the frame on a flat surface.
—Center the imaged transparency face down on the frame and secure all four corners.
—Turn it over so it is face up and check to see if the material is straight and not too close to the edge of the frame.
—Turn it face down again and tape all four edges.

OVERLAYS

Excellent for building a visual's story step-by-step. Information which can be broken down into component parts can be effectively presented this way. It involves the use of two or more imaged transparencies laid over each other which then project as a single image. A transparency may have multiple overlays in:

—FIXED SEQUENCE
When all the overlays are affixed to the same edge of the frame and can only be laid over the base in one sequence.
—RANDOM SEQUENCE
Each overlay must be affixed to a different edge of the frame. May be laid over the base in a variety of sequences.

Attach the overlays to the front of the frame in one of the following ways:

—Use hinges which can be purchased to secure the visual to the frame.
—Use the do-it-yourself stapled folded tape method.
Cut a piece of mending or packing tape 2" long. Affix 1/2" on the underside of the overlay sheet, fold the tape in the center (1") and stick the sides together. Affix the last 1/2" to the top of the overlay above the 1/2" already attached to the underside. Staple the 1/2" protruding beyond the overlay to the transparency frame.

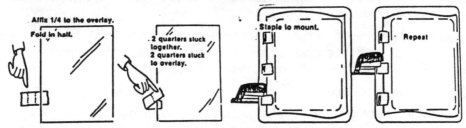

—Use tape as a hinge. Affix the tape so half is on the overlay and half is on the frame so it can be folded back easily.

BILLBOARDING

Highlights a specific area on a visual. A sheet of imaged or unimaged color film is taped to the frame over the base transparency. The section over the area to be highlighted is cut out of the color film with a pencil knife. Be careful to cut only the color film, not the imaged visual.

MASKING

A method for progressively revealing information on an overhead. At the beginning everything on the transparency or appropriate parts of it are covered. Masks are removed when applicable material is being discussed.

—Can be made cheaply from scrap cardboard
—Notations, key ideas and questions can be written on the mask
—Masks are attached to the front of the frame, using tape as a hinge
—Masks can cover a full or partial area, be made like an accordion, use strips, or be circular. They can slide, flip-flop, or reveal one line at a time.

FIGURE 6-4

TRANSPARENCIES — TAMING THE TECHNOLOGY
VOLUNTEER MANAGEMENT PROFESSIONALS
ANDY HART

MATERIALS

FILM

FOR PLAIN PAPER COPIERS
—Designed to work in specific machines. Some need a white sensing strip, while others do not. Copiers using a dry toner require a different film from those using a liquid toner.
—Most available in black image on clear film or black image on colored film.
—Preframed — available for most dry toner copiers with 11" x 14" or 11" x 17" paper feed for bypass paper feed. Black image on clear film.

FOR INFRA-RED TRANSPARENCY MAKERS
—Available in black image on clear film, black image on colored film, color image on clear film.
—Available in a variety of weights — from 2.0 mil to 7.0 mil.
—Preframed — black image on clear or colored film.

WRITE-ON
—Most transparency marking pens can be used on it. Can create visuals at the last minute or right on the spot.

COLORED ADHESIVE
—Sheets of transparent colored materials which can be cut to any shape and adhered to a positive or negative transparency to provide a for emphasis of image highlights.

BACKGROUND

BILLBOARD
—Highlights a specific area on a visual.

HIGHLIGHT
—Write on this with a special pen and a bright yellow image appears.

REVERSE IMAGE
—Clear image on a red, black or blue background.

OTHER ACETATES
—Can also use such things as treated x-ray film, printer's film, construction plastic, freezer wrap, separator notebook sheets, and sheet protectors for handmade transparencies.

PENS
The most important factor in producing handmade transparencies
—Available in water-soluble or permanent inks and a variety of tips.
—Permanent ink will not smudge when dry.

FRAMES
—Pre-made in cardboard or plastic.
—Can be made with almost any hard cardboard, such as poster board, file folders, soap or cereal boxes.

OTHER
X-Acto knife, pattern tape, transparent tape, burnisher, overlay hinges, clip art and other graphics, blue-lined grid paper, blue pencil, rub-off letters, templates.

FIGURE 6-5

HELPFUL HINTS FOR MANAGING EQUIPMENT
By Andy Hart

1. Be sure the projector is placed for maximum effectiveness. Project at an angle so you can remain in front of the audience while allowing every person an unobstructed view of the screen.

2. Plan for a minimum of 8 feet between the projector and the screen.

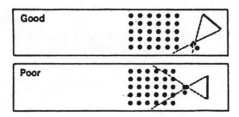

Office/small group arrangement
Project graphics on a light-colored wall or screen behind the speaker.

Auditorium/theater arrangement
For large groups. Discourages discussion.

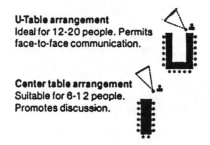

U-Table arrangement
Ideal for 12-20 people. Permits face-to-face communication.

Center table arrangement
Suitable for 6-12 people. Promotes discussion.

Dual overhead projector presentation
Accommodates one or more presenters — one to introduce, one to detail.

3. Keep the position of the screen as high from the floor as possible.

4. Make sure the screen is large enough for transparencies to be easily read by those in the back row.

5. Make sure the transparency is positioned squarely on the screen. (Having them mounted makes this easier)

6. Beware of keystoning. This is a distortion pattern of projected light on the screen which occurs when the screen is not squared with the projector. (i.e.: if the top of the screen is farther away from the projector than the bottom, the light pattern will be wider at the top than at the bottom. This happens because the pattern of light increases in size with increasing distance from the projector).

7. Run a focus check before starting your presentation. If that's not possible, run a check on the first transparency and correct any problems before continuing.

8. Use the overhead projector in a lighted room. That's one of its advantages.

9. Maintain eye contact with your audience. Don't read material from the screen or turn your back to the audience.

10. Use the on/off switch. This allows you to direct attention to either the visual or verbal instruction. Turn off the projector when changing transparencies or when you are through talking about one. This lets the audience return its attention to you. Besides, you blind your audience if you leave the projector on without an image on it. You also lose their interest if you continue to project a transparency once you have stopped talking about it.

11. Sit or stand by the projector. Pacing while the transparency is being projected can be very distracting.

FIGURE 6-6

CHAPTER 7

INDEPENDENT TRAINERS

The information shared in this guide has been deliberately written for either the in-house or independent trainer. At this point, however, I would like to share some tips for the independent trainer specifically. Because I have been in both categories, I can see some differences between the two, and hope my experiences for the last 11 years "on the road" can help you.

STARTING YOUR OWN BUSINESS

It is a big leap from being a trainer working for one organization to starting your own independent training business. It is an even larger leap if you go from being a manager of a program or agency to exclusive work as a trainer or, as frequently is combined, a trainer and consultant.

Before making such a jump, think carefully about several aspects of the training game:

1. What is your greatest strength from which others can learn (product)?

2. Who needs your training (potential clients)?

3. What is your training worth to clients (price)?

4. How would you have to market your training (promotion)?

5. Where are you willing to go to offer your training (place)?

6. What time, money, and energy are you willing to devote to training (resources)?

7. What returns do you need to have and by when (income)?

8. What additional efforts might add to this income (expansion)?

PRODUCT

Too often, people thinking of going into training try to offer too many subjects to clients, with the assumption that by doing so, they will have more opportunities to train. This is correct in the short run, as you will have more jobs at first, but in the long run, you may be hurting yourself because your training is not professional enough to have clients re-book or recommend you to others.

Rather than trying to be a jack of all trades, I urge you to zero in on one, two or possibly three things you do very well and concentrate on doing such a great job with those that people are clamoring for your training!

As you look out into audiences, always remember that those people are potentially your "agent publics," people who can speak on your behalf to others, marketing — or de-marketing — your services. If those folks like you and believe you have something valuable to say, they will tell others, thus setting a climate for possible future work by you. If, on the other hand, they feel you are less than prepared, knowledgeable or enthusiastic on a training topic, they will probably either avoid mentioning you as a possible future trainer or, worse yet, discourage others from hiring you.

In choosing your initial subjects, consider:

1. What am I the most knowledgeable about?

2. What am I the most passionate about?

3. What topic offers me the best and most war stories?

4. What topic offers me the opportunity to relay specific "how to" information?

POTENTIAL CLIENTS

In addition to the above list, factor in what the salability might be for any training you develop:

1. What training is needed? How do you know this?

2. What competition exists around this topic?

3. How easy is it to explain your training product?

4. How accessible are these potential clients to you?

It is not enough to simply be a good trainer offering good training, you must also have a potential client that wants and needs that product AND is accessible to you. Recently my business partner and I have decided to offer some specialty training geared to specific audiences. We recognized that our business background would afford us a good product, complete with experience and war stories, in about six different areas (military, private voluntary organizations, membership associations, private charities, education and church).

In selecting our target audiences, we eliminated several immediately (church, education) because we do not have personal or professional close ties with them. We are now exploring our contacts within the remaining four to assess which might be most likely to offer entry to us for our marketing efforts.

We also assessed which products we offer might be most needed, then prioritized this list by audience and greatest need. We examined competition to see how many firms or individuals are now offering the same product and discovered two topics that no one was offering to two of our target audiences. Obviously that positioned those two potential audiences high on our list of possible prospects. When we have assessed our contacts, we will have our top target clearly in mind and begin to lay out marketing plans to introduce ourselves and services to selected groups.

As you can see, there is a lot of background work that goes into decisions on what to offer and to whom it is offered.

PRICE

Another factor to consider before you begin to set up a training business, is what the market will bear as to fees, costs, etc. After choosing your target audience for your best product, find out what others charge for such training. Talk to potential clients and ask them directly if X training is worth X dollars to them (don't worry, they will be frank!).

DAILY FEES

The going rate for trainers beginning training seems to be about $500-700 for a full day plus expenses. Some trainers start lower, some higher, but this is the range I hear most frequently for those working in the nonprofit sector.

In the profit sector, fees often begin at about $1,000 per day and work their way up quickly. Nonprofit fees tend to stay the same for a longer period.

HOURLY RATES

You may wish to set an hourly charge and work from that. This is true for training, plus consultation and materials development, two natural off-shoots of training. You may even break down consultation into two categories: on site and back in your office. The same sub categories might be true for material development.

Again, in the nonprofit sector, $50-100 per hour is not unusual for consultation or material development done on a client's site, with $25-$50 for work done in your own office. Hourly training fees are typically $100 per hour in larger cities, less in smaller or rural areas. Work in any of these categories for the profit field varies so dramatically that on any given day you will probably find two trainers offering essentially the same effort to two different clients for anywhere from $50 to $300 per hour or more!

FEE LIMITS

Do some careful research about fees you can and must charge for your work. I urge you to place a bottom limit on your fee structure or come up with a sliding scale with which you feel comfortable AND THEN STICK TO IT! Being negotiated down to half what you feel the effort is worth will probably stick in your throat about half way through the work, making it more difficult for you to complete.

Look at the long term relationship you might want with a client and consider your fee structure accordingly. You may wish to offer a lower priced training at first with the understanding that if it becomes a product the organization wishes to use in the future, there will be a different pricing schedule. You also may wish to consider a single price for a package of services such as training, assessment and materials.

NEW PRODUCTS

When trying out a new training product, I often offered it first to a local group at no cost just so I could have audience feedback to use in toning and refining content. I preferred to do this rather than a ridiculously low fee that future local groups would expect.

Believe me, if you are just starting out, one of your biggest challenges may be charging a fee for services. Especially if you have worked in the nonprofit or public sectors of work. Just take a deep breath, tell potential clients your fee and, if they faint dead away, you might wish to adjust it downward a bit or decide that you'll hawk your wares elsewhere!

PROMOTION

I've never understood why this happens, but frequently, a trainer goes to all the hard work to develop a product, research potential clients and set a very fair price and then sits back and waits for the world to beat a path to their door.

It just doesn't happen that way folks!

MARKETING PLAN

You will have to promote or market your services to the potential client you have targeted. Decide on the best way to have contact with groups or organizations and create a marketing plan that lays out:

1. Who the target is.

2. What you have to offer them.

3. What you need/want in return.

4. When you can offer it.

5. How it can best meet their needs.

6. What validity you personally and the training itself can offer.

7. Who you will contact first to try to sell the training.

8. When you will contact them.

WRITTEN MATERIALS

Have written materials to take to potential clients. Even consider a blanket mailing to which you will make follow-up calls in person. (In person approach is always best if possible; phone calls are next best; a letter alone is too easy to overlook or discard.)

BROCHURE

Take care in designing your brochure or marketing letter. Make it:

1. Easy to read — use simple wording.

2. Have it professionally laid out so it is visually appealing.

3. Offer pertinent information:

        a. what you offer.

        b. who you are.

        c. how it will benefit them.

Try to avoid pricing on written materials. You want to be flexible on this and not have your brochures, etc. out of date too quickly when you raise or change costs.

Consider using a photo on your brochure. Surveys tell us people feel more connected to such materials and tend to trust the sender more. Avoid "new age" language unless you specifically want to attract people who consider themselves part of "new age" thinking.

Continually seek ways to promote your offerings in creative and realistic ways. You may wish to advertise in newsletters of groups, companies, etc.; speak at large conferences to acquire high visibility; arrange media interviews; ask to speak at Board meetings to acquaint people with services you can offer, etc. Be creative! Be persistent!

PLACEMENT

Where you are willing to train must become a factor as you look at setting up a training and consulting business. Do you wish to train only at a local level? County? State or Province? Region? Country? or will you go anywhere in the world?

Think about this carefully before you start to market yourself. I once formed a partnership with a gal who was (and still is) a terrific trainer. We began our work and after about three trips around the country, she called me from a small airport in a western state where she was stranded for three hours and sadly announced that the life of the traveling trainer was not for her.

I've heard a lot of such stories from people who had never considered how hard a life that can be. Rushing for planes, eating hot dogs in airports, grappling with brief case, luggage and training supplies, waking up in Ralph's Not So Cozy Motel in Nowheresville to find the only restaurant in town is closed for remodeling.

If you have decided to become an independent national trainer because of the glamor and rich life, I suggest you check your blood sugar level. It may have caused some fuzzy thinking and delusions that have no connection to reality!

If you do wish to travel away from home, decide if there are limitations around that decision. Do you need to limit it to X days per month? Do you want to only piggy back trips into one week per month? Do you need to avoid weekends or a religious holy day in each week? As you consider this, do not forget to factor in travel days. Being from Illinois, if I schedule a full day in California, it really means three days of my time – a day going, a day training or consulting and a day returning home. (I do not charge a fee for travel days, but many trainers do; it is perfectly ethical in most people's minds.)

Consider the WHERE of your training business carefully. Involve those other people in your life that would be affected by your being on the road so that it becomes a decision owned and realistically looked at by everyone.

If it will affect family members, co-workers, partners, etc. have frank discussions around how everyone feels about your absence. Identify methods to lessen any negative impact and be creative with solutions. If you are a parent, consider allowing your children to mark out dates of school events, birthdays, etc. that you agree to NOT be gone for; if you are married or have a significant other, identify dates and events important to them that you will be home for or negotiate something that is acceptable (possibly taking them on the trip and extending it a day or two for private fun); if co-workers are going to have an increased load of work while you are away, find ways to reduce the strain on them. In other words, consider others as you map your own course and draw those "others" into the decision making and negotiation for the best of everyone!

RESOURCES

A sixth factor to consider as you set up in the training business centers around the issue of resources — time, money and energy.

TIME

How much time will you put towards your independent training? Will you begin part time and gradually work toward full time, or will you try to keep it at a part time level? Many people have creatively used vacation time from their full time job to begin a training business, using days off to offer workshops. Could that be the best idea for you?

MONEY

Frequently the second aspect of the resource question, money, will determine the time you can give to training and the overall timeline for entry into your own business. If you are dependent on your income from an existing job, you will need to map out an approach that eases you from your present work into your own company as income from the latter increases.

It is best to have a substantial safety net of money behind you that can ease financial tight spots if you plan a short transition to full-time training. If that cushion is not there, you will have to carefully plan for how you can best meet your financial needs as you move toward independence.

As for how quickly that will happen, there are so many variables that must be factored in. No one can really give you a hard and fast answer. A rule of thumb that seems to apply to new businesses is that in the first year you will have a negative cash flow; the second you may break even, and the third begin to realize a profit.

In setting up my business, I needed to shorten that scenario, and to facilitate that goal, I worked to reduce my overhead or initial outlay of money to a minimum. I created an office in my own home, met needs of duplicating, printing and computing by hiring the work out; kept accounting and record keeping to the simplest formats possible asking for advise from experts;

shopped extensively for best prices on goods or services, and used part-time high schoolers when I needed help in the office.

KEEP IT SIMPLE

By so doing, I avoided office rent, major equipment costs, full time salaries plus benefits, and other items that could be slashed from my start up budget. This reduced my overhead to bare bones and allowed me to see profit after only 10 months. I have maintained this stance of low overhead through 11 years of work and have a business partner with the same conviction, so that now, though we are the largest producer of goods and services in the volunteer sector of the nonprofit world, I still am in a home office (a 1200 sq. ft. addition that appreciated the value of our house) with a part-time Administrative Assistant (15-20 hrs. a week) and consultants in tax matters, accounting, typesetting, design and computerization. We have three specialty printers who have representatives assigned to our accounts: One for printing of books, one for printing of our catalog and the third for miscellaneous printing (newsletters, handouts, etc.). We now rent warehouse space for all our publishing titles, but that is the only "rent" we must shell out.

Because I am infrequently on the road anymore, I am in the office full time to see to the management of the business and have watched our income quadruple in the three years since I began to attend to the management end of our efforts. My partner, Steve McCurley, is on the road for over 100 workshops each year, and we have 12 other trainers to whom we refer business when we can't or don't choose to accept a training contract. We have made a conscious decision NOT to bring on training associates or employees, and instead tap the rich resource of trainers/consultants on a sub-contract or, 99% of the time, a courtesy referral basis.

My point here, is to urge you to keep your business as simple and uncomplicated, both financially and effort-wise, as possible. Plan your transition to full-time training, if that is your goal, carefully and on the timeline that best fits your needs. Involve those significant others who will feel the effect of your financial shift in the decision making so that the plan you map out belongs to everyone.

Realize that starting and maintaining any business is energy draining. You must make all the decisions; to get started and gain visibility you may decide to book yourself very tightly; you never really escape thinking about work, etc., etc. Also, do not be fooled by the easy style many top trainers project from a stage — training is hard work physically, mentally and emotionally. Traveling is exhausting and frequently frustrating and working hard to land a contract, then seeing it slip away, can be discouraging.

All the work you put into developing training, materials, marketing and management of your business does not have a pay check involved and there is never time and a half for overtime! You will have to create your own benefit package of insurance, etc. and all of that takes energy.

Look closely at how hard you want to work. If the load seems more than you want to bear, you may wish to only train part time locally and retain another salaried position that affords both an economic base and benefits.

INCOME

In the exploration of resources, you will need to put some exact figures down on paper as to what you need financially and by when. Consider your start up and continuous costs over the first year. Then factor in your fee structures and how much income would need to be generated each month. Is that realistic against the research you have done on availability of clients who need and can pay for your services?

You may wish to set a time limit by which XX income will be generated by your training and have a contingency plan for what you will do if that level is not reached by your deadline.

Assess your basic needs (not wants or discretionary income) for living, business, etc. and work backwards from that figure. How quickly do you need to generate an income level to cover all those costs? Do you have a source of backup funds to ease you over the first months? When would that backup fund dry up?

Think carefully, and realistically, about income needs and what levels must be reached at what checkpoints along the path to your independent training efforts.

EXPANSION

The eighth factor for you to consider as you set yourself up in the training business is what options you might have to expand your income base. Are there other services you could offer and for which you are equipped? Consider:

1. Consulting.

2. Material Development.

3. Design of organizational instruments (surveys, reports,etc.).

4. Research and analysis.

5. Teaching at local colleges or technical schools.

6. Contracting yourself to a Seminar organization (i.e.: Fred Pryor Training).

7. Offering services based on your unique talents (video taping other trainers, creating visuals, etc.).

What about products?

1. Writing a book or monograph to sell at your trainings.

2. Agreeing to sell books of other writers and retaining a percentage.

3. Developing and then renting a mail list to others.

4. Creating products your target audience needs (clip art, posters, etc.).

I urge you to explore options you have to bring in added income. I personally suggest to trainers just coming into the field to look at a subject that can be worked into a book or monograph. It can be created economically, serves as an added income source and is a constant marketing piece for the trainer. My company now publishes over a dozen newer trainers' works in a cooperative that shares expenses and affords writers a higher return of sales handled from our office that is much better than the 10% offered in standard publishing contracts. Everyone wins — the trainer has a good product without the hassle of self-publishing, we have a wider variety of products to offer our buyers and potential clients have more information from and about a bevy of new faces!

PARTNERSHIPS

To Partner or Not To Partner, That is the Question!

I am frequently asked by newer trainers if it is best to strike out singly or in partnership with others. They want me to choose one of two options, and I probably frustrate them when I respond with the non-answer: "Whatever works for you!"

I've worked alone and tried three partnerships, two of which did not work. I prefer to work with someone else, especially with the size of my business, but realize that may not be the best way for others.

If you do decide to work with others, talk about your working relationship, avoid tight legal contracts and do it as simply as possible. I personally believe that there are two ingredients that must exist before any partnership, formal or informal, will work: TRUST and COMPATIBILITY. Sub heads under these two would be: flexibility, ethics, topics, complimentary skills and goals . . . you might add others as you see fit.

One thing I believe CANNOT be present for any joint effort to be successful is a TOTAL NEED FOR CONTROL. If one person feels the need to call all the shots, review every detail, or have the final say in every decision, you might as well take down your shingle and cut it in half between your two names.

Partners, I believe, have to agree on who does what, then let go of control of what the other is doing, having faith in their competence, skills and good judgment. This means that you let go of believing that every effort emanating from your joint partnership will be exactly as you would have done it if you were the sole proprietor. It won't, but see that as a strength, not a weakness.

If you and your partner are different personalities, GREAT . . . you will probably attract more clients depending on which style they prefer. Keep in mind that partnerships that succeed usually do so because those involved were not trying to be identical clones, but to compliment each other. I've seen more trouble in those joint efforts by people too SIMILAR than I have those of folks who are DIFFERENT.

If you and another professional trust each other, have like goals and definitions surrounding quality, work well together, and compliment each other, explore gently whether a partnership might benefit you both. Don't jump into it, try it out on specific projects. If that feels good, increase your joint efforts, though still allowing for individual efforts for each partner. Avoid tying each other up or putting restrictions around your effort such as: "Neither partner may accept independent training contracts without involving the other." YUCK.

Do not even THINK of hooking up with anyone who plays games, demands their opinions be the only right way to do or interpret things, engages in power struggles, or is inflexible. If even a hint of "score-keeping" ("I had six training jobs last month and you only had five, so I should get to take home more money" or "I counted, and there are 23 more words in our brochure about you than me.") raises it's ugly head, confront it as you move toward the exit.

In short, partnering is a delicate business. Like any close relationship, it depends on the partners commitment to making it work, and must rely on feelings more often than contractual agreements. Sometimes a match that works for many years, suddenly begins to not work for some mysterious and complex set of reasons. When this happens, celebrate the years it was great and move away quickly so that all those good times are not tainted by negativism or hanging on beyond the time when each of you should move on to a new relationship apart from one another.

My final word on partnerships: When they work, don't analyze them to death. Just enjoy and grow. When they don't or cease to work, move out of them kindly and with good wishes for each other. The key to success? MATURITY THAT CELEBRATES SHARED, POSITIVE POWER and TRUST, TRUST, TRUST!

CONCLUSION

Starting and operating a successful training business is a challenging and rewarding career choice. If planned, organized and directed well it will be a great source of growth, satisfaction and learning for yourself and your clients. We are caught in the swirl of the Information Age and are witnesses to exploding change around this little blue planet we call Earth. Our "backyards" extend all the way to lands of very different cultures and beliefs, but the need for learning can be found in every one of them.

I urge you to pursue your dream of training and equipping others to be the best they can be . . . to bring enlightenment, hope and confidence to people wherever they are and to be able to feel the incredible high that comes from making a difference in the lives of others who, in turn, can then be equipped to make our little blue speck in the cosmos a better place for everyone.

Enjoy the journey. Have faith in yourself, your product and the great good sense and kindness of your audiences. Be prepared, wear comfortable shoes, be kind to people, avoid garlic and heavy sauces, laugh at yourself but never others, hang in there by taking time to refresh and renew yourself frequently, and enjoy!

Oh yes, and one more thing: Have 5,000 business cards printed with your name and:

"HAVE FLIP CHART — WILL TRAVEL"

END NOTES

CHAPTER 1 —

1. Jeff Brundney and Mary Brown, *Survey On Volunteer Training* (Athens, GA: Univ. of Georgia, Dept. of Political Science, May 1990)

2. *Webster's New Collegiate Dictionary*

3. Ida Rush George, *You Can Teach Others* (Workshop manual)

4. Malcolm Knowles, *The Modern Practice of Adult Education: Andragogy Versus Pedagogy* (La Jolla, CA: University Associates)

5. Elaine Yarbrough, PhD and Paul Freidman, PhD, *Training Strategies From Start to Finish* (Englewood Cliffs, NJ: Prentice Hall, 1985)

6. *You Can Teach Others*

7. Ibid.

8. Abraham Maslow, well-known quote

CHAPTER 2 —

9. *Trainer Competencies* (American Society of Training and Development)

10. *Training Strategies From Start to Finish.*

11. Vivian Buchan, *How to Read Body English* (Voluntary Action Leadership, 1979)

12. Trudy Seita, *Communications: A Positive Message From You* (Downers Grove, IL: Heritage Arts Publishing, 1989)

13. Adapted from *Training Strategies From Start to Finish*

CHAPTER 3 —

14. Harriet Naylor, *Volunteers Today: Finding, Training and Working With Them* (Dryden, NY: Dryden Associates, 1973)

15. Ibid.

16. *The Modern Practice of Adult Education.*

17. *Volunteers Today.*

18. Ibid.

CHAPTER 4 —

19. *Volunteers Today*

20. Steve McCurley and Rick Lynch, *Essential Volunteer Management* (Downers Grove, IL: Heritage Arts Publishing, 1989)

21. *American Heritage Dictionary*

22. *Essential Volunteer Management*

Chapter 5 —

23. Arlene Schindler, PhD and Dale Chastain, *Primer for Trainers* (1978)

24. Ibid.

25. Ibid.

26. Sue Vineyard, *Evaluating Volunteers, Programs and Events* (Downers Grove, IL: Heritage Arts Publishing, 1988)

BIBLIOGRAPHY

Communication: A Positive Message From You. Seita, Trudy. Heritage Arts Publishing, 1807 Prairie, Downers Grove, IL 60515.

Essential Volunteer Management. McCurley, Steve and Lynch, Rick. Heritage Arts Publishing, 1807 Prairie, Downers Grove, IL 60515.

Evaluating Volunteers, Programs and Events. Vineyard, Sue. Heritage Arts Publishing, 1807 Prairie, Downers Grove, IL 60515.

Facilitation Community Change: A Basic Guide. Fessler, Donald R. University Associates, La Jolla, CA, 1976.

How Adults Learn. Kidd, J.R. Association Press, NY.

How to Read Body English. Buchan, Vivian. Voluntary Action Leadership, 1979.

Human Communication Handbook: Simulations and Games. Ruben, Brent D., and Budd, Richard W. Hayden Book Co., Inc., Rochelle Park, NJ.

Introduction to Group Dynamics. Knowles, Malcolm and Hulda. Association Press, NY.

Making Meetings Work, A Guide for Leaders and Group Members. Bradford, Leland P. University Associates, La Jolla, CA, 1976.

Planning, Conducting and Evaluating Workshops. Davis, Larry N. and McCallon, Earl. Learning Concepts, Austin, TX, 1974.

Presentation Technologies magazine. Lakewood Publications, 50 S. North St., Minneapolis, MN 55402.

Primer for Trainers. Schindler, Arlene, PhD and Chastain, Dale. 1978.

Selecting and Developing Media for Instruction. Anderson, Ronald H. ASTD, Madison, WI.

Survey On Volunteer Training. Brundney, Jeff and Brown, Mary. Athens, GA: Univ. of Georgia, Dept. of Political Science, May 1990.

The Management of Training: A Handbook for Training and Development Personnel. Otto, Calvin P. and Glaser, Rollin O. Addison-Wesley Publishing Co., 1970.

The Modern Practice of Adult Education: Andragogy Versus Pedagogy. Knowles, Malcolm S. University Associates, La Jolla, CA, 1970.

The Role Play Technique, A Handbook for Management and Leadership Practice. Maier, Salem, and Maier. University Associates, La Jolla, CA, 1975.

The Training Store catalog. Training Resource Corp., 5 S. Miller Rd., Harrisburg, PA 17109.

Training magazine. Lakewood Publications, 50 S. North St., Minneapolis, MN 55402.

Training and Development Handbook, A Guide to Human Resource Development. Craig, Robert L., Editor. American Society for Training and Development. Madison, WI, 2nd Edition.

Training Strategies from Start to Finish. Yarbrough, Elaine, Ph.D., and Friedman, Paul Ph. D. Yarbrough Associates, 1113 Spruce St., Boulder, CO 80302.

Websters New Collegiate Dictionary.
. . . .

Also: **Sue Vineyard** has written several new books since The Great Trainers Guide first came out. They include:

> ***Megatrends & Volunteerism: Mapping the Future of Volunteer Programs.*** 1993.
> ***101 MORE Ideas for Volunteer Programs.*** Oct. 1995
> ***STOP MANAGING VOLUNTEERS! New Strategies for Volunteer Program Executives.*** Spring 1996.

Previous books by Sue Vineyard:
Marketing Magic for Volunteer Programs. 1985. 1996. Rev.
Beyond Banquets, Plaques & Pins: Creavtive Ways to Recognize Volunteers. 1989. Rev.
101 Ideas for Volunteer Programs. 1987.
101 Tips for Volunteer Recruitment. 1989.
101 Ways to Raise Resources. 1988.
Evaluating Volunteers, Programs & Events + REFLECTION: the Evaluative Component of Service Learning. 1995 Rev.
Managing Volunteer Diversity. 1993.
Secrets of Leadership. 1991.
Secrets of Motivation. 1992.
How to Take Care of YOU, so YOU Can Take Care of Others. 1989 Rev.
(All of the above books are published by HERITAGE ARTS PUBLISHING, Downers Grove, IL)